Twenty 10-Minute Plays for Teens by Teens

VOLUME 3

Smith and Kraus Publishers
Plays, Scenes, and Monologues for Teens

10-MINUTE PLAYS SERIES:
    Vol. 1 *by Kristen Dabrowski*
    Vol. 2 *by Debbie Lamedman*
    Vol. 4 for Kids/10+ Format Comedy *by Kristen Dabrowski*
    Vol. 5 for Kids/10+ Format Drama *by Kristen Dabrowski*
    Vol. 6 for Middle School/10+ Format Comedy *by Kristen Dabrowski*
    Vol. 7 for Middle School/10+ Format Drama *by Kristen Dabrowski*
    Vol. 8 for Teens/10+ Format Comedy *by Kristen Dabrowski*
    Vol. 9 for Teens/10+ Format Drama *by Kristen Dabrowski*

Great Monologues for Young Actors, Vol. I, Vol. II, Vol. III

Monologues in Dialect for Young Actors

Most Valuable Player and Four Other All-Star Plays for Middle and High School Audiences

Multicultural Monologues for Young Actors

New Plays from ACT's Young Conservatory, Vol. I, Vol. II, Vol. III, Vol. IV

Plays of America from American Folklore, Grades 7–12

Seattle Children's Theatre: Six Plays for Young Audiences, Vol. I, Vol. II

Scenes in Dialect for Young Actors

Short Plays for Young Actors, Vol. I, Vol. II

Short Scenes and Monologues for Middle School Actors

The Spirit of America: Patriotic Monologues and Speeches for Middle and High School Students

Teens Speak Series:
    Girls Ages 13–15: Sixty Original Character Monologues
    Boys Ages 13–15: Sixty Original Character Monologues
    Girls Ages 16–18: Sixty Original Character Monologues
    Boys Ages 16–18: Sixty Original Character Monologues

Ten Plays for Children from the Repertory of the Children's Theatre Company of Minneapolis

The Ultimate Monologue Book for Middle School Actors: 111 One-Minute Monologues, Vol. I, Vol. II, Vol. III

The Ultimate Audition Book for Teens: Serie
    Vol. I: 111 One-Minute Monologues
    Vol. II: 111 One-Minute Monologues
    Vol. III: 111 One-Minute Monologues
    Vol. IV: 111 One-Minute Monologues
    Vol. V: 111 Shakespeare Monologues for Teens
    Vol. VI: 111 One-Minute Monologues for Teens by Teens

For more information or to order, visit us at www.smithandkraus.com
or call toll-free 888-282-2881.

Twenty
10-Minute Plays
for Teens by Teens

—— **VOLUME 3** ——

edited by
Debbie Lamedman

YOUNG ACTORS SERIES

A Smith and Kraus Book

Published by Smith and Kraus, Inc.
177 Lyme Road, Hanover, NH 03755
www.SmithandKraus.com

First Edition: September 2006
10 9 8 7 6 5 4 3 2 1
Manufactured in the United States of America

Cover and text design by Julia Hill Gignoux, Freedom Hill Design

ISBN 1-57525-456-5
ISSN 1553-0477

CONTENTS

ACKNOWLEDGMENTS

I would like to offer thanks to the following people
who supported the efforts of this book:

Eric Kraus and Marisa Smith

Carrie Darrow

Penny Irion at Santa Margarita Catholic High School

David W. Green

Susan Eiden

And a special thanks to all the young playwrights
who submitted their work. I applaud your efforts and hope you
will always continue to create new and innovative work.

INTRODUCTION

What you have here is a whole bunch of new plays written by the teenaged playwright. Writing for teens can be difficult if you're no longer of a "certain age." And as much as I pride myself into thinking that I am young and hip and cool . . . the fact of the matter is, I'm not sixteen anymore. That's probably a good thing. But to write material for this age group can be challenging. So I went to the source. The plays found here are written by playwrights fourteen to twenty years old. The subject matters are diverse, the voices are distinct, and the eclectic genres will provide considerable challenges for young actors.

Immediate gratification can be a good thing. If you get bored with a 10-minute play, hang in there, because another one is on its way. It's like switching channels on a television set. However, I feel confident that the plays in this book will not bore you, but delight you. Enjoy reading them, acting in them, and if they inspire you, you might find yourself writing one of your own!

Debbie Lamedman

CAMP MAZEL TOV

6M, 3F

By Nathalie Kohen
Laguna Beach High School
Laguna Beach, California

Characters

MENDEL: Camper. Cynical, apathetic to camp.
SHMUEL: Camp counselor. Depressed, overexerts himself.
SHEILA: Camp counselor. Stressed, frantic, nerdy.
REBECCA: Camper. Jewish American Princess; bossy.
SHARONA: Camper. Rebecca's sidekick; ditzy, nerdy.
ELI: Camper. Sarcastic.
JACOB: Camper. Weird, horny.
YOSI: Camper. "The good Jew"; always follows rules.
ADAM: Camper. Rebecca's boyfriend; stud, emotional.

Setting

A camp for Jewish adolescents.

CAMP MAZEL TOV

SCENE 1

SHEILA: One summer camp, solitary in denomination
In fair Malibu, where we lay our scene
From Jewish tradition break the unconventional
When hormones possess the selfish teen
From forth the departure of Manischewitz wine
Homesick children await the day
When Hebrew songs are sung in English
And eating is done free of prayer
Does their hunger bury their religious faith?
Or indifference to such bonding days
There is but one reason they do submit
To Camp Mazel Tov's diminished craze
The star-crossed campers, thousands abound
Make their annual glory on holy campground

SCENE 2

MENDEL: *(Robotically.)* But, soft! What light through yonder window breaks? It is the east, and Juliet is the sun. Arise, fair sun, and kill the envious moon, Who is already —

SHMUEL: Stop, stop, stop the scene! Mendel Teitlebaum this is about love! Why are you staring at her breasts? Now look into Juliet's eyes . . . Feel the passion. Try it again. Take it from the top. *(Mumbles.)* We should have done *Fiddler on the Roof* . . .

MENDEL: *(Worse than before.)* But, soft! What light through yonder window breaks?
It is the east —
(Enter Camp Counselor Sheila Horowitz.)

SHEILA: *(Frantically.)* Shmuel! Senior Maccabi is throwing their matzo balls at the Junior Maccabi!

SHMUEL: Are they doing that damn initiation again?

SHEILA: I think so. We have to hurry. Little Yentel and her sisters are starting to look like dinner, and Michael Bruchim just lit the papier-mâché menorah on fire!

SHMUEL: The chutzpah! Mendel, Sharona, Rebecca, Yosi, Eli, Jacob—stay here. Look over your script and get it right. I'll be back in a minute.

(Exit Sheila and Shmuel.)

SCENE 3

REBECCA: I'm not going to stay here. I could be with my boyfriend. Besides, Eli, you smell.

ELI: I'm sorry we can't all be Rebecca Miller — The Rabbi's Daughter.

REBECCA: My father isn't a rabbi idiot. He's one of the most respected cantors in all of Los Angeles!

JACOB: Who's the boyfriend this week, Becky?

REBECCA: Adam Cohen

JACOB: Which one? There are five . . .

REBECCA: Brown hair, tall, pasty, smart, rich. *(Smiles at Sharona.)*

MENDEL: That narrows it down

REBECCA: Yeah, we are in love. He gave me his bar-mitzvah pendant yesterday. He told me that he loves me. As long as I wear it, I'm his Juliet and he is my Romeo.

ELI: *(Laughs.)* I hope the story ends the same way.

REBECCA: For your information, we are staying together.

ELI: He goes to boarding school in New York.

REBECCA: *(Blatant look.)* Your point being . . . ?

ELI: Boys, I'm out. They are giving away challah rolls by the dining hall.

(Exit Eli.)

SCENE 4

REBECCA: Uch, he is so annoying.

SHARONA: I know. The other day I told him that his green polo didn't match his blue pants and he laughed at me.

MENDEL: They were jeans, Sharona.

SHARONA: So? Blue and green obviously clash.

REBECCA: OK, so I was thinking I should make Adam a card.

SHARONA: For what?

REBECCA: He's leading the boy's Senior Maccabi Shabbos service tonight!

(Sharona looks at her questioningly.)

REBECCA: I want to wish him good luck!

SHARONA: Can I come help?

REBECCA: If you promise not to tell everyone that we hung out. Jacob, darling, will you be a doll and tell Shmuel the Mule that we went on a run to the bathroom if he comes back?

JACOB: *(Doubtfully.)* Yeah, but uh, what's going on in the bathroom? What are the girls doing in there?

(Exit Rebecca and Sharona.)

SCENE 5

MENDEL: Rebecca is so hot.

JACOB: Yeah, but she's a JAP.

MENDEL: Clearly. JAPs are hot.

YOSI: I think you meant to say Jewish American Princess, but nonetheless using the word JAP can be highly offensive to Jews and to the Japanese.

JACOB: I think Jeff Goldblum is hot.

MENDEL: The actor?

JACOB: Yeah.

MENDEL: Well . . . he's married.

YOSI: Well, only for religious purposes *(Giggles.)*

JACOB: Do you think Shmuel is coming back?

MENDEL: I hope not. I'm sick of playing Romeo. I didn't even
choose drama as my elective. I wanted Israeli dancing. Jacob,
we should go. Shmuel isn't going to come back in a long
time. The Junior Maccabi are going through initiation; you
remember how long that takes?

JACOB: Yeah, they spent an hour watching me dance the hora
in my underwear in the girls' cabin.

YOSI: They should have been kicked out of camp for that!

JACOB: It's OK. I'll do it when I'm a senior.

YOSI: I won't. I'm not going to ruin the healthy Jewish experience that these kids should be having.

JACOB: The hora is a Jewish experience.

YOSI: I'm going to get ready for dinner. Don't be late. Shabbos
services start at seven-thirty tonight!

SCENE 6

JACOB: Let's ditch services tonight and go through the girls'
cabin.

MENDEL: Why would I do that?

JACOB: Dude, the girls' cabin . . .

MENDEL: Point being . . . .

JACOB: *(Angrily.)* Does there always have to be a point with you!?
Gosh.
(Exit Jacob.)

SCENE 7

Mendel gets up to leave. Enter Shmuel.

SHMUEL: *(Out of breath.)* OK guys, I just settled everyone with
the matzo balls; Yentel and her sisters are fine — Mendel,
why are you the only one left?

MENDEL: I think they're all in the bathroom *(Begins to leave.)*

SHMUEL: Where are you going?

MENDEL: The bathroom

SHMUEL: OK, well hurry back. Tell the others that they need to come back in five minutes.

(Exit Mendel.)

SHMUEL: *(Depressingly.)* I spent four years at Yeshiva University. I spent another four years at Yale. Forty thousand dollars times eight! And what do I get for eight years of tests and three hundred and twenty thousand dollars? Shakespeare and matzo balls! I try my hardest to give these kids the Jewish love they deserve. Three years at Camp Mazel Tov, and I'm still just "Shmuel the Mule"! It's a sick world with teenagers, especially Jewish ones.

(Exit Shmuel.)

SCENE 8

Enter Rebecca and Adam Cohen. They are giggling behind the curtain.

ADAM: No one's in the drama room.

(More giggling, and Rebecca bites Adam's tongue.)

ADAM: Ouch!

REBECCA: What?

ADAM: *(As if he had a speech impediment.)* You bit my tongue.

REBECCA: Oh, sorry.

ADAM: Let's make out in here.

REBECCA: Right, but Adam, say it to me once more.

ADAM: *(Pause.)* Uhhh . . . let's make out in here.

REBECCA: No, I want to hear you say what you said before that again. Three words that ring a bell . . .

ADAM: *(Thinks.)* You bit my tongue?

REBECCA: Adam, that's four words. Your father doesn't send you to private school for nothing.

ADAM: I honestly don't know what you want to hear from me,

Rebecca. One day you want to hear me say how fat you are, the next day you want to hear me say how skinny you are. Then you ask me to tell you how real your Tiffany's bracelet looks . . .

REBECCA: It is real!

ADAM: Like I said, it's real!

REBECCA: Are you trying to tell me that I am wearing knockoffs?

ADAM: No, I'm not saying that. I was using it as an example.

REBECCA: You know what, Adam? I'm going to go. When you remember what it was that you were supposed to say to me, you know where to find me.

ADAM: Where?

REBECCA: Ugh!

(Exit Rebecca.)

SCENE 9

Enter Jacob and Eli.

JACOB: (Walking into drama room.) OK, so at eight o'clock when services start, we'll raid the girls' tent.

ELI: Yeah, but which one?

JACOB: We'll choose the messiest. Messy girls are hot.

ADAM: I think Rebecca just broke up with me.

ELI: Why?

ADAM: I think it was something I said . . . or didn't say.

ELI: Make it up to her

ADAM: (Depressed.) I don't know what she wants from me. She wants me to be her Romeo or something. Something with three words . . .

ELI: Get Mendel to help you. He's great with Shakespeare.

ADAM: I think that's what she wanted. Chicks like Shakespeare. She probably meant something about Romeo, Romeo, where for art thou Romeo?

JACOB: That's six words

ADAM: We can cut it down to three. Think it might work?

ELI: Sure man. I'll get Mendel. Sit tight.

    (Exit Eli.)

JACOB: So what were you guys doing in here? Making out?

    (Enter Mendel.)

ADAM: Mendel, buddy! I need a favor.

MENDEL: Yeah, what?

ADAM: I need to say a really nice poem to Rebecca so that she'll take me back. Like, Romeo and Juliet or something.

MENDEL: Take my part in the drama production.

ADAM: And then what?

MENDEL: Well, uh, when your line comes that starts with "Juliet is the east," replace Juliet's name with her name. *(Chuckles.)*

ADAM: But then Romeo will fall in love with Rebecca. Rebecca's mine.

MENDEL: You want her to like you, right?

ADAM: Yeah

MENDEL: Then just listen to me. Do it for your own sake.

    (Exit Mendel, Jacob, Eli, and Adam.)

SCENE 10

Next day at rehearsal.

SHMUEL: *(Tired.)* Where's Mendel?

ADAM: He's in the bathroom. I'm going to fill in for him today.

SHMUEL: Who are you? Never mind, I don't even care anymore. Let's just get the scene done. I just want to . . .

REBECCA: If you think that walking in on me acting is going to make me like you again you can . . .

ADAM: *(Passionately delivered.)* But, soft! What light through yonder window breaks?

It is the east, and Rebecca is the sun.
Arise, fair sun, and kill the envious moon
(Pause.)

REBECCA: Oh, Adam! I love you! My little mensch!

SHMUEL: Baruch hashem! Baruch hashem!

YOSI: The messiah!

(Cast sings song and sways while holding hands. Mendel walks past stage without notice.)

MENDEL: A glooming peace this morning with it brings;
The sun, for sorrow, will not show his head:
Go hence, to have more talk of these sad things;
Some shall be pardon'd, and some punished:
For never was a story of more woe
Than this gift from God
Camp Mazel Tov

END OF PLAY

BETWEEN MOTHERS AND DAUGHTERS

2F

By Caress Zepeda
California High School
Whittier, California

Characters

MOTHER (DANA): Late thirties; typical stressed-out mom; tired with dark circles under her eyes, hair a little messy; clothes look a little dated.

DAUGHTER (ALEX): Sixteen years old; typical angry teenage girl; dark eyeliner and shadow, lip piercing, hair in face; ripped jeans, tank top, and a worn navy hoodie.

Setting

A therapist's office with a desk, couch, and chair. The therapist desk is right in front of the audience, making the audience the therapist. Daughter will lie on couch and talk; Mother will sit on chair and talk.

Mother is sitting in chair in front of desk. Daughter ~~ ~~.,~~g~~ on couch behind and to the right of Mother. Cue lights to shine on each character only when they speak.

MOTHER: *(Very loving, proudly.)* When I was pregnant with my daughter Alex, I was so excited. I couldn't wait for my little girl to arrive. I would stare at the calendar and cross off each day that passed until she was born. I knew I would be a wonderful mother and that my little Alex would love me as much as I loved her. We were gonna be best friends!

DAUGHTER: *(Irritated.)* Your mother cannot be your best friend. What was she thinking? Do you really think that your mom can understand you? Yeah, my mom said I could come to her for advice or to talk, but whenever I do, she flips out and yells at me for dumb things . . . Oh, and that whole . . . *(Sits up.)* "I was your age once" speech is pretty old. I know she was my age, duh, but like twenty years ago! The world is a totally different place! She might as well as have grown up on a different planet! Gosh! *(Slams back down on the couch.)*

MOTHER: Ha. Alex knows she can trust me! I always try to give her advice, but when I sit her down to talk, it's like she doesn't listen. She must tune me out or something because I'll advise her against something, and she'll do it again. She just doesn't listen. You know, that's the problem with Alex . . . *(Yells.)* SHE NEVER LISTENS! Not to anyone who tries to guide her correctly. Nope, she only listens to her friends or her music.

DAUGHTER: Do you really want to know what my mom's problem is? She judges everything I do! If I don't place first in track or don't get like, straight A's, she freaks out! I hate that she is constantly telling me . . . *(Sarcastically.)* "You know you need to give it your all, try harder" or "You better clean up your act missy." Why can't it be, "Wow, Alex, second place, you did great!" I don't even know why I bother even trying anymore . . . *(Screams.)* NOTHING I DO IS GOOD ENOUGH FOR HER!

MOTHER: *(Rests head on left fist.)* I'm telling you that girl has to get her act together. Oh, let me tell you about this one little incident. I was waiting for her to come home after school, and it was five-thirty, and she hadn't even called to let me know she wasn't going to be home by three. So I jumped in the car and started towards her school . . . *(Getting worked up.)*

I was driving around for fifteen minutes before I saw her. Do you know where she was? She was sitting on a trash can in some rundown alley with that no good friend of hers, Rhonda. *(Leans closer to the desk and whispers.)* I've heard bad things about that girl.

(Normal voice.) They were watching some filthy looking boys jump around on skateboards! I could not believe that *my* daughter stayed out to do this! Why does she hang out with kids who most likely know the principal's office like they know the back of their hands? My little angel, being corrupted by those little . . . little hoodlums.

DAUGHTER: *(Hands on face.)* Oh my gawd! *(Stands up and paces around the office.)* That woman is psychotic! This one day I was hangin' out with Rhonda and the guys after school, and I told Mom that I was gonna be home by six. So anyways, we were just watching the guys skate, you know, laughing, having a great time when I see my mom's little turd-on-wheels. She starts to scream her head off, and she is saying all this nonsense, in front of *all* of my friends! I was ready to die, it was so embarrassing! She seriously needs to learn how to chill out. I mean, hello, I'm sixteen, what does she want me to do, stay at home with her all day? *No way!* I like to hang out with Rhonda and the rest of them. I like to go out and have fun. She just completely overreacts. *(Sitting comfortably.)* Man, you should have seen her when I got my lip pierced. *(Smirking.)*

MOTHER: *(Horrified.)* Did you see what she did to her face? She is so beautiful, and she goes and ruins her face with that thing in her lip! Now she's going to get a scar that will remind me of it every time I look at her. She got punished big time for that one. No phone or online privileges for a month. I even picked her up straight from school.

DAUGHTER: *(Nonchalantly.)* So I got my lip pierced, who cares? I didn't think it was a big deal, but I guess I forgot that Mother is overdramatic. I got grounded for a month.

(A little agitated.) She took away my phone rights and unplugged the computer. When I walked out of my school's gate I would see the turd-mobile parked right in front. For a month, I was my mother's prisoner! *(Defiantly.)* It's my face, it's my decision if I want to have a lip ring or not. I'll take it out when I'm good and ready to.

MOTHER: *(Defensively.)* I just don't want her to regret her mistakes. I want her to get help before she becomes even more brainwashed and out of control.

DAUGHTER: *(Scratches head.)* I don't even know why I'm here. I'm not the crazy one, she is! "Dana" has been acting like this since . . . well, I guess since Dad left. *(Concentrates and says softly.)* Yeah, that's when she got all weird.

MOTHER: I think she started acting up when her father left us four years ago. She probably told you it was my fault that her dad is gone. She gave me a bad time about it a few times before when the money situation was still being settled. We had to struggle for a while. He was our only support. I didn't have to work when I was with him, and he left so suddenly, it was a while before I could get work. *(Welling up.)* I didn't even know what to tell Alex when she asked why he left. I tried to explain, but I . . . I couldn't even convince myself.

DAUGHTER: *(Clearly upset now, getting uncomfortable.)* He didn't even tell me why he was leaving me. We had a great life with him, you know, like a TV family. We had a nice house and a great car, not like the apartment and turd parked down there. No, and we used to do all this fun stuff. Why would you even want to leave all that? *(A tiny smile emerges.)* I remember when he took me to the zoo. We would always see the monkeys first, and he liked to save the lions for last. He always bought me a pretzel and any souvenir I wanted. Mom took me once, right after he left, to take his place I guess. It wasn't the same, but . . . *(Smiles gone and tears begin.)* she's all I got now.

MOTHER: *(Crying.)* I wish she could see that I try my hardest to do everything I can for her. I want her to have nice things and to live in a better city. I just want her to appreciate what I do for her. I want her to learn responsibility and to do good in school. I want her to grow up and be successful. I want her to be able to depend on herself and not be stuck depending on a man. *(Shakes head slowly while saying.)* She shouldn't have to struggle the way I do now.

DAUGHTER: *(Lots of tears.)* I know my mother works hard, I appreciate that, I appreciate everything she does. She has to see that I am gonna make something with my life. I'm not gonna end up a housewife and depend on a man. I know I can only depend on myself and no one else. Mom has aged so much from working, and she's always tired and I . . . *(Points to self, angrily.)* could be doin' more around the house for her. I . . . *(Shouting, points to self.)* CAN STOP ASKING HER FOR MONEY AND STUFF I DON'T NEED. I love my mom. *(Sobbing uncontrollably.)* I need her.

MOTHER: *(Sobbing.)* I love Alex with all of my heart. I'd do anything to make her happy. I just want her to be happy with life and with me. *(Takes tissue and wipes tears.)* I want to be the best mother I can for her. But being a mother . . .

DAUGHTER: And being a daughter . . .

TOGETHER: *(Both walk up to the desk.)* . . . is so hard.

(Lights go out.)

END OF PLAY

IM

2M 2F

By Andrew Levy
United Nations International School
New York, New York

Characters

JOHN: A teenager, dressed in jeans and T-shirt and wearing a leg brace.

ALTER-JOHN: An actor, hunkier than John, dressed the same as John but with no leg brace.

SARAH: A hot blond: the kind whose hair shines even when she doesn't use conditioner; dressed in jeans and a tank top.

ALTER-SARAH: An actress, looks the same as Sarah and dressed the same.

Setting

Two desks with computers, facing each other. The desks are in two "separate" bedrooms; each pair of actors at each computer terminal cannot see the other pair.

IM

At rise, John, a pale teen, sits in front of a computer monitor, hunched over a keyboard. Spotlight is on him, typing intently. Light comes up on Alter-John, standing slightly up stage. His pose is slightly unnatural, like an unstrung puppet. John sighs and clicks keys as lights come up on Sarah. Alter-Sarah is standing in front of Sarah's computer. John begins to type. The audience doesn't know what he is typing until Alter-John speaks the words John types.

ALTER-JOHN: . . . and so the guy was singing "I'd rather die happy, than not die at all."

ALTER-SARAH: *(Giggles as she types.)* LOL. Isn't that from some old song?

ALTER-JOHN: It was on of one of my dad's tapes.

ALTER-SARAH: You listen to your *dad's* music.

ALTER-JOHN: *(Turns to address typing John.)* Careful, Dude. You could blow this.

ALTER-JOHN: Uh, no. Not really. Though he's pretty cool . . . you know . . . for a dad. But I can live with that. So how have you been?

ALTER-SARAH: I turned seventeen last week.

ALTER-JOHN: Hey, that's great! Happy birthday. Did you party it up?

ALTER-SARAH: Yeah. Me and some people went out to a club. We got sooo drunk. I had a lot of fun! Some guy on the lacrosse team and I made out so much! But he makes out with everyone, so I guess it isn't special. So have you gotten into any sports?

ALTER-JOHN: No, I haven't. *(Turning to John.)* OK, no. That's not a way to get with a girl. Man, for her, you are on every team in your school. *(Turning back to Alter-Sarah.)* Yeah, I've been getting into some teams.

ALTER-SARAH: *(To Sarah.)* Hmmm . . . I don't know, Sarah. Sounds like he's fronting.

SARAH: He sounds totally hot!

ALTER-SARAH: That's so cool! What teams?

ALTER-JOHN: I'm getting really into my soccer . . . and my volleyball.

ALTER-SARAH: You must be a ladies' man, am I right?

ALTER-JOHN: Yeah. But it depends on what ladies. Ha, ha.

ALTER-SARAH: *(Giggles before typing.)* You are like the funniest person I know.

ALTER-JOHN: Really?

ALTER-SARAH: Totally. I am just about rolling on the floor laughing.

ALTER-JOHN: *(Smiling. To John.)* Dude, you're waiting too long. Capitalize on your success man. *(Snaps his fingers.)*

ALTER-SARAH: Hello? You there?

ALTER-JOHN: Yeah, I'm here.

ALTER-SARAH: Good. I don't want to be alone right now.

ALTER-JOHN: Why? Is something wrong?

ALTER-SARAH: It's a *long* story.

ALTER-JOHN: Well, I've got a while. Let's hear it. If it's not too personal.

ALTER-SARAH: Well, me and my boyfriend Tom have been going out for a long time, and . . . wait, do you promise not to tell?

ALTER-JOHN: Pinky swear.

ALTER-SARAH: OK. So I was going out with him for a long time. And I thought he was the one, you know? And I felt so happy with him, I wanted him to be the one to take my virginity. So I . . .

ALTER-JOHN: So did he? *(He's shaken by this line of conversation. Out of his depth.)* Take your virginity, I mean.

ALTER-SARAH: Maybe, if you let me finish the story you'll find out.

ALTER-JOHN: Oh, sorry. Keep going.

ALTER-SARAH: So I was walking home from school with him a

few days ago, and this other girl was walking with us. When we got to Tom's house, she went in with him. He said she needed to pick up a book from his house. So I went on home, and they went in together. I finished my homework a few hours later and went to Tom's house to surprise him. I knocked on his door, and he didn't answer, but I saw a light on in the window, so I went over and looked inside.

ALTER-JOHN: And? Was he there?

ALTER-SARAH: Yes. And he was sitting on his bed with the other girl. Kissing.

ALTER-JOHN: But did she get it? *(To John.)* Get what?

JOHN: The book. Did the girl get the book she came for?

ALTER-JOHN: I am not saying that to her. This girl is sizzling, and if you say that you can forget about ever getting with her.

ALTER-JOHN: I'm sorry. That guy sounds like a jerk. He doesn't deserve you.

ALTER-SARAH: That's sooo sweet! So how about you? Are you single?

ALTER-JOHN: *(To John.)* Wait. Before you say anything, think this through. We are in dangerous territory. We could make a move, or we could play out the sympathy thing and hope she takes the bait. Don't tell her that you've never had a girlfriend. Say you've just gotten out of a bad relationship. And say that you don't think you're ready for another girl. Girls totally dig that crap. Actually, why don't you leave this to me? I'll handle it. I'm not letting *this* one get away.

(John starts to type. Alter-John shakes his head slowly.)

ALTER-JOHN: Yeah, my last girlfriend was playing on me too. I didn't know if I could handle it. Actually, I still don't know. I just want a girl who I can care about and who cares about me.

ALTER-SARAH: You're so deep! I thought all guys were after was sex.

ALTER-JOHN: Well, that's not all we are after. LOL.

ALTER-JOHN: *(To John.)* Shut up! *(To Alter-Sarah.)* Yeah, if only there was a girl who felt the same way as me, then I would have all I need.

(Sarah types. Alter-Sarah seems worried and fretful. Sarah watches passively.)

ALTER-SARAH: Oh, my God. You are the sweetest guy I have ever met. You will definitely find a great girl.

ALTER-JOHN: I think I just found one.

(Sarah leans out from behind her computer and looks at John, who is doing likewise. Alter-John looks worried and angry.)

ALTER-JOHN: Goddammit, John! Shut the hell up! Why can't you just let me do this? I'm trying to get you some ass, man! I am calling the shots now!

JOHN: *(John looks from Sarah to Alter-John and stands up shakily.)* No, you're not! You're just using me! Without me, you can't do anything! You aren't helping us. You're helping you! *(John points to his keyboard.)* I can destroy you right now without even thinking about it.

ALTER-JOHN: *(Alter-John cackles wickedly.)* I don't think so. *(Alter-John walks over to John and pushes him away from the computer. He then sits down at the keyboard and types while he speaks to John without looking his way.)* When you used me to get close to people online, you believed in me. It was all you had. It was pathetic. I don't need you, loser.

(John hangs his head. Sarah watches this turn of events calmly but attentively.)

ALTER-JOHN: So . . . *(Turning to Sarah.)* Hey, let's go somewhere, eh? *(Winks.)*

ALTER-SARAH: Yeah, sure.

(Alter-John punches John on the arm and walks past Alter-Sarah to Sarah. He holds out his arm, and she links arms with him. As they exit, Sarah hesitates.)

SARAH: Who is that?

(Alter-John turns to look at John, who is on the floor crying.)

ALTER-JOHN: Oh. It's nobody. Nobody important.

(Alter-John and Sarah exit. John lies back on the floor and tries to control his breathing. Alter-Sarah looks at him and sits down at Sarah's computer. She types while she speaks.)

ALTER-SARAH: John? Are you there?

(John sits at his computer, wiping a tear from his eye, and begins to type.)

END OF PLAY

THE WOMAN FROM FARGO

4M 3F

By Lanna Jackson with TeeJay Gaskill and Liz Williams
Trollwood Performing Arts School
Fargo, North Dakota

Characters

WOMAN
YASH
REID
LIZ
BROOKS
TEEJAY
RACHEL

Setting

A middle-aged woman sits on a park bench.

THE WOMAN FROM FARGO

Lights up on Woman sitting on a bench reading. Yash enters. He is East Indian. He sits. Awkward silence.

WOMAN: *(Thick Norwegian accent.)* Well, you don't look like you're from around here.

YASH: Actually, I was born here. My parents are from India, though.

WOMAN: Oh, you're an Indian! How!

YASH: What?

WOMAN: How!

YASH: How . . . how am I an Indian?

WOMAN: No! How . . . hi! You know, your word for hello.

YASH: My word? Um, I think you're a little confused . . .

WOMAN: Well, you're an Indian, aren't you? Instead of hi, you say how! So, how!

YASH: I find that really offensive.

WOMAN: Oh, settle down, Temper-Like-Bear. I have to say, I loved your people in *Dances with Wolves*! And that Kevin Costner is such a stud muffin! Now I've always wondered, where are the restrooms in your teepees?

YASH: Are you kidding me? I can't believe you just . . . forget it. I'm out of here.
(He exits.)

WOMAN: Have a nice pow-wow! Well, he was nice for a savage!
(Enter Reid.)

REID: *(With a British accent.)* Excuse me, but might I sit?

WOMAN: Well, sure!

REID: Thank you! *(Big smile.)*

WOMAN: Why, your teeth aren't bad at all!

REID: Um, thank you?

WOMAN: They're so straight and white and everything.

REID: Why wouldn't they be?

WOMAN: You know, I always thought that it was all the tea that stained your teeth like that. You must have paid a lot to get them bleached and straightened.

REID: Madame, if you are inferring that just because I'm English I have bad teeth, then you are . . .

WOMAN: Now, how is the queen these days? She must be upset with all the turmoil in that family right now.

REID: You are terribly rude! I hope you get mugged!
    (He exits.)

WOMAN: Cheerio! Those Brits are so polite!
    (Enter Liz. She sits.)

LIZ: Hi!

WOMAN: Hello! My goodness, what beautiful hair! Is that a perm?

LIZ: No actually, it's natural. I get it from my dad's side of the family.

WOMAN: What do you mean?

LIZ: He's black.

WOMAN: No, you're too light to be an African American!

LIZ: Actually, I'm mulatto.

WOMAN: Is that a skin disease?

LIZ: No! It means that my dad is black and my mom is white.

WOMAN: *(Gasps.)* My goodness! That's terrible!

LIZ: Excuse me?

WOMAN: And just think! They had a child! Scandalous!

LIZ: That is so eighteenth century! I thought people were over that.

WOMAN: They shouldn't be over it.

LIZ: You shouldn't be allowed out of the house!
    (She exits as Brooks enters.)

WOMAN: Hi there! Would you like to sit?

BROOKS: Sure.

WOMAN: So, where are you from?

BROOKS: Winnipeg, actually.

WOMAN: I knew it! You look like a hockey player.

BROOKS: I do? I thought I looked smart.

WOMAN: I don't get it. Oh, that must be that French humor. Goodness, I bet this heat is just killing you.

BROOKS: Not really.

WOMAN: Of course it is! Up there it's winter all the time. This 65-degree weather is probably a heat wave!

BROOKS: Actually . . .

WOMAN: Now, where is your sled team?

BROOKS: My what?

WOMAN: Your dogs and sled? How else do you Canadians travel around up there?

BROOKS: Lady, I take a bus! God!

(He exits as Teejay enters.)

TEEJAY: Can I sit?

WOMAN: Well, sure! So where do you go to school?

TEEJAY: North.

WOMAN: That's nice. What sports do you play?

TEEJAY: None this year. I'm doing theater.

WOMAN: Theater? Like musicals?

TEEJAY: Yeah, some . . .

WOMAN: You must be one of those homosexuals!

TEEJAY: What?

WOMAN: Do you know that you are going to hell? Being gay is a sin! These days, people just keep turning gay. It's a terrible epidemic!

TEEJAY: What do you mean, turning gay?

WOMAN: Well you gays are infecting everyone! Liberace, Elton John, Tom Cruise . . .

TEEJAY: Just because I'm in theater doesn't mean . . .

WOMAN: I'll pray for your soul, if you still have one.

(Teejay leaves. Enter Rachel. She sits.)

WOMAN: I should write that down. Let's see . . . *(Woman is digging through her bag.)* Hmmm . . . excuse me, do you have a pen?

RACHEL: A what?

WOMAN: A pen.

RACHEL: A pan? You want a pan?

WOMAN: Ya, you know, to write with.

RACHEL: Lady, that's a *pen*! A *pen*! God, you North Dakotans. None of you know how to speak.

WOMAN: Excuse me?

RACHEL: No, it's fine. You probably lost your pen in the minivan on the way to church after picking up your three kids from soccer practice.

WOMAN: Young lady, I . . .

RACHEL: Save it, Mary Beth. Go make a hot dish.
(She exits.)

WOMAN: *(Stunned.)* I can't believe that she made those assumptions about me! It is so rude to think those things based only on appearance. She must be a Democrat!

END OF PLAY

POP CULTURE IS AN ANARCHIST

2M or 2F or 1M, 1F

By Jillian Gates
Santa Margarita Catholic High School
Rancho Santa Margarita, California

Characters
CAITRIN
CLARE

Setting
Caitrin and Clare sit in an empty movie theater.

Note: The two characters are given female names but can be played by either gender.

POP CULTURE IS AN ANARCHIST

The lights come up and music plays softly as if the feature presentation has just ended.

CAITRIN: That was . . .

CLARE: Yeah.

CAITRIN: No, I mean . . .

CLARE: I know.

CAITRIN: We should . . .

CLARE: Tell someone?

CAITRIN: What do we say?

CLARE: What can we say?

CAITRIN: It was just a movie.

CLARE: Yeah, but it was . . .

CAITRIN: They carded you at the theater door. They weren't going to let you in.

CLARE: They had to let me in.

CAITRIN: You're seventeen.

CLARE: I'm seventeen.

CAITRIN: They asked you when your birthday was.

CLARE: Do I really look that young?

CAITRIN: That's hardly the point. Don't you see? They knew.

CLARE: Knew.

CAITRIN: Knew that this shouldn't be seen.

CLARE: It has to be seen.

CAITRIN: This film is going to start . . .

CLARE: Start a revolution.

CAITRIN: I feel brainwashed.

CLARE: There was definitely subliminal messaging.

CAITRIN: Were we supposed to root for the bad guy?

CLARE: Yes.

CAITRIN: But he blew up Parliament!

CLARE: But just think if he hadn't.

CAITRIN: Shouldn't some British man somewhere be concerned about this? I mean, hell, people got pissed when they blew up the White House in *Independence Day,* and those were just f'ing aliens. This stuff's got us talking terrorists.

CLARE: Anarchists.

CAITRIN: Terrorists!

CLARE: If enough people saw this movie all at one time — I think there'd be a f'ing revolution, man.

CAITRIN: Of what sort? And why?

CLARE: Don't you get it, man? If we don't reform the way we live in this world, we're going to regress to f'ing . . .

CAITRIN: World War II.

CLARE: The f'ing Holocaust!

CAITRIN: But it gets worse.

CLARE: Much worse. Hell, we'll regress until a civil war destroys us.

CAITRIN: This is ridiculous! It was a movie!

CLARE: Could you feel the strong Nazi undertone? I mean, the dictatorship, the concentration camps?

CAITRIN: Yeah, but I mean we just have to look at this whole thing as some young hotshot director taking his opportunity to raise enough conflict out of his film that everyone will see it. That's all it is.

CLARE: So we're just supposed to ignore the whole message of the film?

CAITRIN: I'm not even sure what the message was! Are you?

CLARE: No, but I think it was strategically laid out that way. We're not supposed to remember.

CAITRIN: So, we're just supposed to go blow up some national monument? For what? What's the purpose?

CLARE: No, that's not the point!

CAITRIN: Then what is the point, Clare? Huh? What is the point?

CLARE: Oh, my God.

CAITRIN: Jesus. What now?

CLARE: Look what it's done to us. I mean, we're yelling. This could constitute an argument.

CAITRIN: Yeah, so? We're obnoxious teenagers. That's what we do.

CLARE: OK, yeah. But take this on a larger scale. If this happened to every innocent moviegoer that saw this film . . .

CAITRIN: We'd all be at each other's throats . . .

CLARE: And about what?

CAITRIN: I don't know.

CLARE: Don't you see?

CAITRIN: What's happening?

CLARE: This was all planned out.

CAITRIN: We're paranoid.

CLARE: Someone wanted us to think this way.

CAITRIN: Are we on drugs?

CLARE: No.

CAITRIN: Should we be?

CLARE: It all starts here . . .

CAITRIN: Oh, God.

CLARE: We are the future.

CAITRIN: This conversation is inane.

CLARE: Do you want to see it again?

CAITRIN: The movie?

CLARE: Yes.

CAITRIN: Now?

CLARE: Yes.

CAITRIN: I do.

CLARE: Me too.

END OF PLAY

LOVE AND WAR

6M 2F

By Kaitlynn Maggi and Jessica Walden
The California Conservatory of the Arts
San Juan Capistrano, California

Characters

RUBY: Nineteen-year-old girl in 1942, just got married to longtime boyfriend George; sweet.

GEORGE: Nineteen-year-old boy in 1942, newly wed to Ruby; brave, masculine.

KRISTEN: Nineteen-year-old girl in 2003, first year in college; strong willed, but sweet and smart.

JACKSON: Kristen's boyfriend of five years, first year in college, studying to become a teacher; kindhearted, not nearly as tough or manly as George.

ARMY OFFICER 1: George's officer.

ARMY OFFICER 2: Jackson's officer.

DOCTOR 1: Ruby's doctor.

DOCTOR 2: Kristen's doctor.

Setting

The two scenes are played simultaneously: one set in 1942, the other in present day.

LOVE AND WAR

Lights come up on Ruby waiting, looking out down stage right. George enters.

GEORGE: Ruby? Oh, Ruby!

RUBY: *(Turns to see George up left.)* George! *(Runs and jumps into his arms. They both begin to cry and kiss. Blackout.)*

KRISTEN: *(Lights come up on Kristen, down left, on cell phone.)* Yes . . . I waited for everyone to get off the plane. He's not on it! They just said to come and see if the person I am expecting comes off the plane . . . they wouldn't tell me anything else. WHAT IF HE'S GONE MOM . . . what if he's — *(Cut off.)*

JACKSON: Kristen . . .

KRISTEN: What? Jackson! . . . *(She turns around, realizing what she just said.)* JACKSON?
(She drops her cell phone. Jackson drops his luggage, and they run toward each other. She jumps into his arms, and they kiss. Blackout.)

SCENE 2

After a fun night dancing, George confronts Ruby.

RUBY: What would I ever do without you, George? Tonight was so wonderful.

GEORGE: Ruby, I love you, you know this . . . but there's something I have to show you.

RUBY: What George? *(George hands her the letter.)* No. George! You can't, George. *(Starts to cry, opens the letter.)* I don't know what to say. What am I supposed to do? Well, I guess now is a good time to bring up *my* news. *(Holds stomach.)*

GEORGE: Oh, Ruby. *(Holds her.)*

(Lights come up on Jackson and Kristen walking in.)

KRISTEN: Jack, what's going on? *(Still enjoying the music.)*

JACKSON: I pulled you out here, because I need to tell you something.

KRISTEN: Jackson, why tonight? Don't be ridiculous, let's just go back inside. *(Grabs his arm going to leave.)*

JACKSON: *(Pulling her back.)* Krista, really.

KRISTEN: Jack! . . . OK . . . well . . . what is it?

JACKSON: *(Pulls out letter.)* I don't know where to begin, so I guess I will just start by saying, I didn't choose this.

KRISTEN: Jack, just tell me. *(Grabs letter.)*

JACKSON: I'm going into the army. It's a draft letter.

KRISTEN: What? I don't understand.

JACKSON: I signed up a while ago, not thinking anything about it. They need me Kristen.

KRISTEN: Stop kidding around . . . I thought you were propos — no . . . What about me, Jackson? What's going to happen to us . . . What the hell am I suppose to do?! I can't believe this. *(Exits, furious.)*

JACKSON: Kristen! Wait, please!

SCENE 3

Lights come up on Ruby, as she begins monologue to her unborn baby.

RUBY: How could he do this to us? To you . . . you aren't even a part of our world yet, and he is leaving. I'm sorry. Things were going to work out perfect, now I have to raise you on my own. I'm scared . . . I'm so scared. I always thought that as soon as someone got married, the army would just skip over you, because they knew your love was serious . . .

serious enough to bring a baby into the world. I guess that's not reality. Don't they understand what they are doing? They are taking away your father! *(Collects herself.)* It's going to be OK; it has to be. He is fighting for our country, and that's what is important. I will manage without him, until he returns . . . But what if he doesn't? What do I tell you? How will you take this news? That you never met your father? This is happening too soon, I'm not ready for this!

GEORGE: *(Offstage.)* Ruby! Are you ready?

RUBY: *(Takes deep breathe.)* I'm ready. *(Lights go out, Ruby exits.)*

(Lights come up; Kristen begins her monologue.)

KRISTEN: Oh, God. What am I going to do? I'm going to tell him, that's what. No . . . no I'm not. What am I supposed to say? Oh, by the way Jackson, I'm pregnant . . . we aren't married . . . our parents would flip . . . you are going to war . . . and I'm going to raise the baby by myself . . . see you in a couple years! Don't be ridiculous, Kristen . . . I need to talk to someone . . . but I can't talk to my parents, they would probably pass out . . . if I tell one of my friends, they will just spread it like wildfire . . . It'll ruin my reputation . . . if I have the baby . . . I will have to go to college with . . . a baby . . . or not even go . . . we're not ready for a baby . . . *(Looks down and then picks up a pamphlet on abortion.)* I never thought my life would come to this. *(Begins to cry.)* I love him . . . but I can't have this baby.

JACKSON: *(Offstage.)* You ready, babe?

KRISTEN: *(Hides pamphlet, wipes her tears.)* Yeah, I'm ready . . .

SCENE 4

Lights go up on George and Ruby. It is their last good-bye.

GEORGE: I will write you as soon as I get there.

RUBY: Promise?

GEORGE: *(Holds her chin so they make eye contact.)* Promise. I love you, Ruby . . . *(He kisses her and rubs her stomach.)*

RUBY: *(Begins to cry.)* I love you, George.

(Lights go out. Lights come up on Kristen and Jackson.)

JACKSON: Are you OK . . . you've been quiet since we left the house.

KRISTEN: *(Checks back into reality, after staring off to space.)* What? . . . yeah . . . I'm fine.

JACKSON: So . . . I guess this is it.

KRISTEN: How cliché! No it's not . . . *it* . . . I'll see you soon. *(Begins to laugh, then starts to cry.)*

JACKSON: Kristen . . . don't cry . . . please.

KRISTEN: I know. *(Wipes tears.)* It's just hard, you know.

JACKSON: Of course, I do. I love you, Kristen.

KRISTEN: I love you, too.

(They kiss, lights go out.)

SCENE 5

Jackson and George are lined up right next to each other, but the scene plays out as one scene. Lights go on one person every time he speaks, otherwise blackout. Army Officer 1 and George are responding to each other, and Jackson and Army Officer 2 respond to one another.)

ARMY OFFICER 1: Attention!

ARMY OFFICER 2: Stand up straight, cadet.

GEORGE: Yes sir . . .

ARMY OFFICER 2: WHAT DID YOU SAY? I CAN'T HEAR YOU!

JACKSON: Yes, sir.

ARMY OFFICER 1: Don't think for one minute I will show any sympathy for you, cadet. Do I make myself clear?

GEORGE: Ya . . . ye . . . yes. Yes, sir.

ARMY OFFICER 2: *(Grabs Jackson's shirt.)* I don't take wimps in the army. If you can't manage ME, how are you supposed to manage thousands of bombs going off . . . guns shoot-

ing from every direction? Get your mind off your girl . . .
Or else you won't live to see her again! ARE YOU LIS-
TENING TO ME?

JACKSON: YES, SIR . . . But, sir . . .

ARMY OFFICER 2: WHAT DID YOU SAY? DROP AND GIVE
ME ONE HUNDRED . . . NOW, CADET! *(Officer throws
him to the ground.)*
*(George shows no emotion, while officer starts yelling. Jack-
son starts getting upset, and you can tell he's scared when
officer starts yelling. This should happen simultaneously.)*

SCENE SIX

*(Ruby and Kristen are sitting onstage simultaneously, while
Jackson and George read the letter standing behind their
respective partners. Lights go up on the girls one at a time
when either she or her partner is reading.)*

RUBY: Dear Ruby,

KRISTEN: Dear Kristen,

RUBY: Sometimes I think it is colder without you . . .

KRISTEN: even though it's the middle of summer.

GEORGE: I hope all is well back home.

JACKSON: You would think the army would be more welcom-
ing . . . it just makes me think how much I want to be with
you . . .

GEORGE: and our soon-to-be-baby. The training is like nothing
I've ever experienced.

JACKSON: People are dying right in front of my eyes, and we
aren't even in battle yet. Fears I never thought would sur-
face are overflowing my mind.

GEORGE: You shouldn't worry though, I am doing just fine. Even
though it's hard here, I know I will get through it. I have
to get through it.

JACKSON: Have I already mentioned I love you and miss you?
Because I do, and I'm sure the guys have heard how much

I care for you one too many times. I hope you are managing school OK.

GEORGE: I hope the family is well, and oh, your birthday!

JACKSON: Happy nineteenth my love! Thank you for the letters.

GEORGE: Your scent reminds me so much of the times we spent together.

JACKSON: The little moments in our day that make everything worthwhile.

GEORGE: Our wedding. I hold your picture close always, and there is not a moment that goes by without thinking about you.

JACKSON: I know this whole thing is hard, but I hope you can forgive me and be proud of your soldier.

GEORGE: I hate this part, but if I am to die, I want you to continue on.

JACKSON: Keep me in your heart, but find someone that loves you as much as I do to make you happy . . .

GEORGE: to help raise our child . . .

GEORGE/JACKSON: Good-bye for now my love, but not for long.

RUBY/KRISTEN: With Love . . .

RUBY: George.

KRISTEN: Your brave soldier, Jackson.

SCENE 7

Lights come up on Kristen waiting for abortion doctor.

DOCTOR 2: Are you ready Kristen?

KRISTEN: Yes.

(*Lights go out, Kristen exits. Ruby is now onstage, and lights come up.*)

DOCTOR 1: Mrs. Ruby Johnson . . . it's time . . .

RUBY: (*Fully pregnant, very visible, takes deep breathe.*) OK . . . (*Lights go out, sound of baby crying in background.*)

END OF PLAY

ANGEL, ARE YOU THERE?

1F 1M or 2F (1M Voiceover)

By Christina Martinez
Cypress College
Whittier, California

Characters

SARA: Twenty to twenty-five years old; appears healthy; loyal
fiancée to Kyle.

DEATH: Any age, preferably older, can be played by a male
or female; cloaked, we never see his or her face.

KYLE (VOICEOVER): Fiancé to Sara.

Setting

Sara's bedroom. Exactly four-thirty in the morning.

ANGEL, ARE YOU THERE?

Sara's bedroom. A twin bed is against the stage left wall. Next to the bed is a desk with a chair; an alarm clock and telephone are on it. Up stage there is a door, presumed to be an exit. Another door is stage right, presumed to be a closet. A full-length mirror hangs the closet door. At rise, Death is sitting at the desk, waiting. Sara is asleep in the bed. The alarm begins to buzz as the clock hits four-thirty A.M. The clock will never go past four-thirty A.M., until the very end. Sara is still half asleep as she sits up, hits the alarm clock, and grabs the receiver.

DEATH: *(Interrupting her routine.)* Sara.

SARA: *(Startled and frightened, almost breathless.)* What? . . . Who? . . .

DEATH: Don't be afraid.

SARA: *(Echoing him.)* Afraid . . . Who are you? What's going on?

DEATH: You know who I am.

SARA: I don't understand . . . What? What's happening? Why do I feel so . . . ?

DEATH: Warm?

SARA: Yes. But it's different. It's not just warm. I feel light, like I'm not really *feeling*. What's going on? *(Realizing in a panic.)* Wait. Wait! I have to call him. I have to call my fiancée. He has to go to work. I have to wake him up.

DEATH: Sara. *(Trying to get her to focus.)* Sara, you *don't* have to call him. You've done this every day for the last two years. He doesn't need you to call him anymore. It's time to go, Sara.

SARA: No. No. I have to call him. I have to wake him up. He won't wake up if I don't call him. *(Tears.)* I have to say good-bye. *(Beat.)* I have to say good-bye, don't I? *(Death nods.)* But why? Why? *(Beat.)* I don't understand.

DEATH: Yes, you do Sara. It's time to go. You can say your good-byes. But you don't get to come back. This is it. I'm here to take you, Sara.

SARA: But *why*? I'm only twenty-four years old. I have to get married. *(Softly to herself. Crying slowly.)* Kyle. *(Beat.)* We're supposed to get married! I want a baby. Start a family. *(Beat.)* I'm only twenty-four.

DEATH: No, Sara. *(Beat.)* I'm here because you were *sent* for. I know this is not easy to understand, but it's time for you to take your place.

SARA: I was *sent for*? Why? What *place*?

DEATH: Sara, everything you have ever learned in your life has been true. Everything you have been taught, everything you have come to understand has been Truth. *(Beat.)* Do you understand you are not just a part of this world . . . you are a part of this Earth. You have been endowed, Sara. Your power of wisdom exceeds that of any other human being.

SARA: So . . . I'm like an angel? *(Death nods.)* Oh . . . So what do I do now?

DEATH: You've done all you can do. Now you have to leave.

SARA: So this is it? This is how it ends? I just die, in my sleep? *(Silence.)* It's a brain aneurysm, isn't it? I can *feel* it. *(Rubs side of head.)* I've always felt it. *(Beat.)* I thought it was just me. I thought that was just how it was. It was like I was watching everyone on fast-forward and . . . and I couldn't understand why they were doing what they were doing. They don't notice me *watching*. I just figured nobody really watched. I didn't know I was an . . . *(Hesitation as if she is afraid of the word.)* angel. I just thought I knew something people didn't. I hated it. I didn't know how to live among these people. I just knew I had to help them. *(Rising out of bed.)* But what if I'm not ready to . . .

DEATH: Sara, you *are* ready to. That is why I am here. This decision does not rest in your hands anymore. It is time for you to accept the destiny you have been honored with.

SARA: What do you mean "accept the destiny I've been honored with"? Don't I have a choice? How is this an honor?

DEATH: Sara, since you were born, you have exceeded the spiritual limits of this world. The contributions you have made on this Earth were unexpected . . . so now you shall receive your reward.

SARA: What contributions? I don't understand. You think taking my life away and handing me a halo is a reward? If I've been endowed with such an amazing amount of wisdom, then why isn't any of this making sense? If this is my *destiny*, then why does this feel so much like a nightmare I can't wake up from?

DEATH: You can't be scared now, Sara. Fear is for those who have been humanized —

SARA: *(Interrupting.)* I don't want to be dehumanized. This is too much for me.

DEATH: I understand this message is not an easy one to receive, but I am here to take you, Sara. It is too late for that.

SARA: Why? Why is it too late? How did I get this?

DEATH: Do you remember Edna? Do you remember Scottie the Sparrow? Have you forgotten Elijah?

SARA: *(Recalling, sitting back down on the bed.)* Edna . . . she, she was my community companion. *(Beat.)* She was my best friend.

DEATH: She was also seventy-two and terminally ill.

SARA: *(Quiet realization.)* I was so young then. I didn't know what was happening to her. *(Beat.)* I can still remember the strong smell of her perfume. *(Remembering the tragedy of her death.)* And I remember how small her funeral was. *(Sobbing.)* Seven people. *(Beat.)* I knew Edna deserved something greater.

DEATH: She got it. But not until she reached the other side.

SARA: The other side?

DEATH: *(Nodding.)* Yes. And that's where Scottie the Sparrow came from.

SARA: But Scottie was just a bird. What could he have to do with this?

DEATH: You kept him alive.

SARA: Of course I did. He was just an innocent bird. I didn't want him to die.

DEATH: *(Profoundly.)* But he wasn't meant to live. *(Beat.)* You see, your love and wisdom is too powerful for this world.

SARA: *(Beginning to understand.)* And that's how I knew Elijah was coming.

DEATH: That's how you knew he needed you. Even then at the age of thirteen, you could sense he was lost.

SARA: *(Remembering with excitement.)* That's right. And it only took fourteen days for us to find his mother. She was all the way down in Tallahassee . . . but we found her.

DEATH: *You* found her. Elijah needed your guidance. Without you, his mother might never have been able to look into the eyes of the child that she had lost so many years before. You saved Elijah, just like you saved Scottie the Sparrow.

SARA: *(Smiling to herself.)* Elijah still sends me a Christmas card every year.

DEATH: I know.

SARA: So all this time . . . I've been living my life and I've been using these gifts . . . these powers, whatever . . . to help people, and all the while I was destined for something else?

DEATH: Something greater.

SARA: Something like an angel? *(Death nods.)* So, what now?

DEATH: Now there is Kyle.

SARA: *(Suddenly realizing she has yet to call and wake him up.)* Kyle! I have to call Kyle . . .
(She reaches for the phone when Death softly catches her by the arm and begins speaking. Sara is a bit shocked by his touch as there has been no contact until this quick moment.)

DEATH: Kyle has been one of your most beautiful miracles. Without you, he may not be *alive.*

SARA: He just needs someone to love him.

DEATH: No. He *needed* someone to love him. Kyle is complete now that you have cleansed his soul and restored his virtue.

SARA: *(Saddened.)* Are you saying Kyle doesn't need me anymore?

DEATH: No. I am saying it is time for you to receive your place. Kyle will flourish. By restoring his faith, you have taught him that he is capable of all that he dreams. You removed the impurities that debilitated his mind and spirit. He was like a puzzle that was beyond the point of completion. And yet . . . you pieced him back together. He was indeed your most brilliant of miracles.

SARA: *(Understanding.)* And that's why you've come now. *(Beat.)* Because Kyle finished rehab and cleaned up his life. Because he's complete . . . *(Beat.)* . . . and now I have to leave him.

DEATH: Yes.

SARA: *(Deep breath, accepting her fate.)* How?

(Death rises from the computer chair for the first time and gestures for her to do the same. Sara rises.)

DEATH: This is an honor of the highest, bestowed upon those who have answered a calling heard only by the soul. Now is a time of embracing. Shed yourself of earthly possessions. Free your mind of fear. Cleanse your soul of negativity. Breathe out the toxins that obstruct your clarity.

(Sara closes her eyes in concentration. She breathes in and out slowly and deeply. Death faces her and ever so slowly moves across the room as she instinctively follows.)

DEATH: Sara, all that you know in this life has been Truth. The light inside of you shines too brightly for this world. You are no longer a part of this world. May you find your place in the Sky.

(The mirror on the backside of the closet has now opened up into nothingness. There may be light radiating from it, or it may just be a hollow darkness. As the mirror moves away, Death steps through it. As we see Sara take her final steps from this world, the phone rings only twice. And as the answering machine picks up, Sara moves through the

open mirror. The clock finally turns to four-thirty-one A.M.
The voice heard on the answering machine is Kyle.)

KYLE: *(Voiceover.)* Angel, are you there? Sara? I just woke up.
You never called me. You always call me. I just wanted to
make sure everything was OK. Well, I've got to get ready
for work. Today's the big day, remember? God, I hope I get
this promotion. Anyway, I'll call you later when I get the
word. I love you . . . bye.
(Blackout.)

END OF PLAY

BEST FRIENDS

1M, 3F

By Taryn Dicterow
Laguna Beach High School
Laguna Beach, California

Characters

MANDY: A carefree, kindhearted, but clueless girl who, over the last month, has started a relationship with Alex.

JULIE: Mandy's best friend for many years and a newer friend of Marissa's. She provides an emotional outlet for the other girls to talk about Alex, though she doesn't like talking about him.

MARISSA: A new friend of both Mandy and Julie (over the last year) who has been close to Alex for a long time, though Mandy isn't aware of it. She has had romantic feelings for Alex for a long time but is afraid to act on those feelings because of her friendship with Mandy.

ALEX: New boyfriend of Mandy, old friend of Marissa. He wants to get more physically close with his old friend Marissa while remaining a "good" boyfriend to Mandy. Opportunistic and amoral, he tries to hook up with both girls at different times.

Setting

The stage is cut in half with separate lighting on either side; the two scenes happen simultaneously.

BEST FRIENDS

Scene 1

At Julie's house (stage left), Mandy and Julie talk about Mandy's new perfect boyfriend. After a while, Julie gets bored of this commentary. At stage right, Marissa and Alex are just hanging out, watching TV, when Alex tries to make the moves on Marissa.

JULIE: So, how was it?

MANDY: What? Oh you mean the date with Alex?

JULIE: Duh, what else? So, what did you do, and more important, what did you *do*?

MANDY: Well . . . we went to dinner and a movie, you know the norm. But it was so cute . . . he was a perfect gentleman. He opened the door for me, and he was so polite, and it was our one-month anniversary, you know, and anyway, he . . .

MARISSA: So, how was it?

ALEX: What? You mean the date with Mandy?

MARISSA: Of course. She's my friend; I like to hear about these things. It was your one-month anniversary, wasn't it? Do anything special for her?

ALEX: *(Annoyed and uninterested in talking about Mandy.)* Yeah, but we didn't do anything special. I don't really want to talk about it. So, *(Looking intently at Marissa.)* what have you been up to lately? It's been a while since we've been able to spend time together. *(Once again annoyed.)* Mandy's always calling me and wanting to get together and . . . taking up all of my time.

MANDY: I still can't believe we're going out. I mean, Alex is always so sweet, and we talk, like, every night.

JULIE: *(Bored.)* Wow, that sounds almost too good to be true. You sure you aren't bugging him?

MANDY: Oh, no, he loves talking to me on the phone and in person and at school. We have this great open relationship; you just don't understand.

JULIE: *(Looking down, filing her nails, under her breath.)* Maybe he's just trying to get in your pants.

MARISSA: Well, don't you like her? She seems to really be into you.

ALEX: I know. I guess she's all right. *(Moving in closer.)* But I like to keep my options open. *(Hinting.)* I guess, if I found someone new, I could always go for her instead.

MARISSA: *(Nervously laughs.)* Yeah, I'll have to keep my eyes open for you.

(Alex attempts to move in closer, but Marissa suddenly gets up, in obvious discomfort. Alex looks up at her in disappointment.)

MARISSA: Who wants popcorn? I know I do. *(Exits.)*

MANDY: Don't be silly Julie; he's not like that. He's kind and caring and . . .

JULIE: Whatever, maybe I'm wrong; but it sounds to me like he's trying to butter you up so you'll be willing to —

MANDY: Julie!

JULIE: Well, it's true. That's all guys think about.

MANDY: Maybe with you, in your deranged relationships, but with us, it's different.

JULIE: Whatever. I — *(Phone rings.)* I have to get that. *(Exits.)*

MANDY: *(To herself, trying to prove Julie wrong.)* I think I'm gonna call him right now; I'm sure he's waiting for me to. *(Alex's cell phone rings; he picks it up.)*

ALEX: Hello?

MANDY: Hey, Alex, it's Mandy, what are you up to?

ALEX: Oh, hey sweetie. *(Looks off for Marissa, and seeing no signs of her return, he continues.)* Oh nothing . . . just uh . . . thinking of you. Why, what are you doing?

MANDY: Oh, nothing, the same. So . . . you're not doing anything tonight?

ALEX: No, I'm not with you am I? So I guess I'm left here at home all alone to think about you.

MANDY: *(Alluringly.)* Well, you could be . . . I mean *with* me . . . if you want to, tonight.

ALEX: Well, uh, there was this special I wanted to see . . . but since I don't really have any other plans, I'd love to get together.

MANDY: Really? Oh, that's great. There's this new movie I really wanted to see about —

MARISSA: *(Off stage.)* So, Alex, you want extra butter with the popcorn as usual?

ALEX: *(Covering the phone.)* Oh, yeah, thanks . . . *(Softer, not covering the phone.)* Mom, you always know how to make dinner the way I like it.

MANDY: Who was that? Was that your mom? It didn't sound like her.

ALEX: Oh, yeah . . . of course, it was . . . who else would it be? She just has a cold, that's all. *(Hearing Marissa returning.)* So, uh, I'll meet you in an hour at Crescent Park, OK?

MANDY: Oh great, that sounds . . .

ALEX: Cool. I'll see you then, bye.

MANDY: Uh, OK. *(Hangs up.)*

(Marissa enters the room with popcorn.)

ALEX: *(Still pretending to be on the phone.)* OK, Mom! Jeez, I'll be home in an hour, we can handle it then! *(Hangs up.)* Sorry about that; it was just my mom. She gets so annoying sometimes.

MARISSA: So, you have to leave soon? That means we can't watch that scary movie on Pay-Per-View. What are we supposed to do now?

ALEX: *(Moving in.)* Well, I can think of something that we could do to . . . pass the time. *(Suddenly kisses her on the lips. Marissa moves away.)*

MARISSA: Alex! What are you doing, we're friends, you and . . . Mandy, you're like, going out, and . . . what was that?

ALEX: I'm sorry. I thought you might want to, you know, be friends with benefits. I'm sorry. If you don't want to *(Knowing she wants to.)*, we can always watch TV or something.

MARISSA: No, I mean, I'm sorry but you're going out with . . . Mandy and we shouldn't . . . *(He suddenly kisses her again as if only to shut her up.)* Do that, I mean —

ALEX: I'm sorry, if you don't want to. I thought that it would be —

MARISSA: *(Hesitant.)* No, it's not that. It's that she's my friend, and your girlfriend. Isn't it cheating? We shouldn't —

ALEX: No. Do you think I would do something to hurt your friendship with Mandy? Never, I just thought it would be fun to —

MARISSA: Really? How is this not cheating if you and I hook up? It's you and another girl together —

ALEX: It's not just any girl, it's you. And it's not like we would be hooking up like some one-night stand, we're friends and —

MARISSA: You really think so?

ALEX: Totally.

(Julie re-enters the room.)

MANDY: *(Sighs.)* I guess I'm gonna have to leave you alone soon. That was Alex. He wants to get together tonight at the park! How romantic is that?

JULIE: Great, really great.

MANDY: Do you think he has anything special planned? Oh, my God! What should I wear?

JULIE: I don't know. What's wrong with what you're wearing now? It looks fine to me.

MANDY: Don't be stupid, Julie. I can't wear something like this in front of Alex. I have to look my best for him. Cute, yet sexy. Casual, but nice. Know what I mean?

JULIE: OK, OK, I get it. But you're over here, you don't have any more clothes with you . . . what, you want to borrow some of mine?

MANDY: Was kinda hoping you'd offer.

JULIE: I wasn't. *(Mandy pouts.)* Whatever. Borrow what you want. But, whatever you do, don't get any stuff on it. They are my clothes.

MANDY: *(Giddy.)* Thank you! *(Running into the closet and getting various things she could wear.)* What do you think about this on me, do you think he would like it?

JULIE: Well, that was my —

MANDY: You're right, it's totally wrong for tonight. Oh! What about this? It would be *perfect.*

JULIE: Sure, fine, whatever, take what you want. *(Under her breath.)* It's not like it's mine or anything.

(Marissa is now sitting on Alex, on the couch, and they are kissing.)

ALEX: *(Stopping to look at his watch.)* Is it that late already? I guess I have to go. I'm sorry. We'll have to do this again though.

MARISSA: *(Getting up.)* You sure you have to leave now? I'm sure your mom can wait just a little longer.

ALEX: *(Looking in the mirror, fixing his hair.)* I want to, really I do. It's just, my mom wanted me home an hour ago when she called, and apparently I forgot to do something important at home. Sorry, —

MARISSA: OK . . . This is our little secret right? You're not going to tell her, are you?

ALEX: Marissa, how stupid do you think I am? I would never do that to you. Plus, it's not like I was cheating. We're simply friends with benefits, right?

MARISSA: Right, but —

ALEX: Don't worry, I don't want you to get caught. I promise I'm not going to say anything.

MARISSA: OK, so I guess I'll see you Monday at school?

ALEX: Right, so uh, bye.

MANDY: Thanks so much for helping me get ready. Oh, it looks like I'm already running behind. Gotta go. See ya later, bye.

JULIE: *(Escorting her out.)* Yeah, bye.

(Mandy exits.)

JULIE: Finally.

(Cell phone rings. Light goes up on Marissa, who is making the call.)

JULIE: Hello?

MARISSA: Hey, Julie, what's up? You doing anything?

JULIE: Was, but now I'm free. You?

MARISSA: Same. So, you wanna do something?

JULIE: Sure, wanna come over?

MARISSA: That sounds great. I need to talk to you about something. You see Alex was just over and . . .

JULIE: He was? That's funny. Mandy just left my house to meet up with him.

MARISSA: *(Shocked.)* She did? Well, anyway, I'll talk to you when I get there.

SCENE 2

Julie's room on stage right and a park bench on stage left. Marissa is coming over to Julie's house to talk to Julie about her boy problems. Alex is intently waiting for Mandy at the park when she finally arrives.

ALEX: There you are. I thought you weren't coming. *(Gets up and kisses her on the cheek.)*

MANDY: Oh, you know me, always late. I wanted to look good for you.

ALEX: Well, you do. So, uh, how come you wanted to get together?

MANDY: Oh, I don't know, I wanted to . . .

ALEX: To . . . you know?

MANDY: No silly, I just wanted to be with you and talk like we always do.

ALEX: Talk, great . . .

JULIE: Hey, so what did you wanna talk about?

MARISSA: It's just. I don't know what to do. You see, Alex was over and . . .

JULIE: Yeah, and you . . . Oh, my God, you didn't! Way to go!

MARISSA: No, not exactly, we just . . . kissed.

JULIE: So, you did do something. Wow.

MARISSA: I know. Is that wrong? He said it wasn't wrong . . . that we were just friends with benefits. But I don't know,

JULIE: It's probably not that big of a deal, don't freak out. You know them, they're always together, but he's not getting any action so . . . maybe he just wanted some from you.

MARISSA: You think? That's . . . all it was? *(Disappointed.)* OK, it's just, I wouldn't have usually done that, you know, unless . . .

JULIE: Unless what?

MARISSA: I kinda like him, a lot. Otherwise, I totally would've pushed him away. We've been friends for so long and . . .

JULIE: Don't worry about it, I'm sure it was nothing. You'll be fine.

MARISSA: I just don't want Mandy to —

JULIE: Don't worry about her, she'll never know, and if she doesn't know, who cares?

MARISSA: OK, but I was thinking, maybe I would tell Mandy.

JULIE: No! You can't do that! She, uh —

MARISSA: Would be really mad, I know but . . .

JULIE: It's not that, it's just . . .

MARISSA: Just what? Why shouldn't I tell her if it won't make her mad? I think I should probably tell her how I feel about him.

JULIE: She won't be mad; she'll be surprised.

MANDY: So, you were just sitting at home by yourself when I called?

ALEX: Oh, yeah, I was just waiting for you.

MANDY: Aw, that's so sweet! But were you reading or something? You couldn't have just been waiting by the phone.

ALEX: What? Oh, yeah, I was reading. Um . . . *Moby Dick.*

MANDY: Really? *(Knowing something is up.)* I heard voices.

ALEX: Did I say reading *Moby Dick*? I mean I was watching the movie. You know, books and me, they just don't go together.

MANDY: Right, whatever, I was just wondering. *(Looking at watch.)* I think I have to go home now; it's getting pretty late.

ALEX: But we've only been here for a few minutes! You made me . . . get out of bed and get dressed to be with you for this?

MANDY: Well, if you weren't doing anything else, this should have been the highlight of your evening.

ALEX: Well . . . it was but, I . . . I just wish that we could be together longer. You know, we've been going out for a month and . . . we *are* all alone.

MANDY: Alex! You'd better not be saying what I think you're saying.

ALEX: What? Oh no, not that. But we . . . we don't spend enough time together, that's all.

MANDY: It's just time you want?

ALEX: Of course. What else?

MANDY: You're right; I don't know what I was thinking.

ALEX: *(Relieved.)* Great, so . . . you can stay.

MANDY: Really, I wish I could, but it is getting late. My mom is gonna be really pissed at me.

ALEX: OK, fine. *(He gets up and kisses her on the cheek. They exit.)*

MARISSA: I think I should tell her because it — it felt right with him. It's probably nothing, like you said, but I really don't feel like it was nothing.

JULIE: Whoa, really? It's too bad they're together; otherwise, it would be a lot easier to be "friends" with him.

MARISSA: About that, I thought that maybe if I talked to her . . .

JULIE: Then you'd get the green light to move in on him? Forget about that; she's crazy about him. Even just now, the whole time she was over, it was Alex this and Alex that.

MARISSA: All right! I get it, she likes him. But that doesn't change the way *I* feel, and I think if I talked to Alex about it, he would say he likes me too.

JULIE: God! What the hell is so special about this guy, anyway? He's not hot, he's not that nice, and neither of you have even done anything with him.

MARISSA: I don't know why Mandy does. It's probably because this is the longest she's ever gone out with anyone without him dumping her. But for me, I've known him forever. We've always been so close, and I feel like I know him on a different level than I know anyone else. This is special.

JULIE: OK, maybe you should tell Mandy. But I'm warning you, this will lead to nothing but hostility between you guys. Two girls over one guy, that breaks up friendships all the time. Is it even worth it?

MARISSA: I don't know. On the one hand, there's this guy . . . that I've known forever. A buddy, and now, maybe even more. On the other hand, there's this friend, and friendships last forever. That is if something stupid, like this, doesn't get in the way.

JULIE: Then I think you answered your question. This is enough Alex for me tonight. I think you should go home and try to think of something to do before Monday, OK?

MARISSA: It looks like I've got some thinking to do, but I wish that she didn't like him so much.

JULIE: But she does. *(Trying to nudge Marissa out.)*

SCENE 3

Two lunch tables on either side of the stage, separate lighting. Mandy and Julie are talking at one table, while Alex is alone, for a brief while, at the other. Marissa nervously walks over to Alex from off stage.

MARISSA: So, Alex?

ALEX: Oh, hey girl, what's going on? I had fun this weekend.

MARISSA: Yeah, about that, I did too. But, I just don't feel right about that whole thing. I don't think we should do that again, at least not keep it a secret.

ALEX: What? Like, you wanna tell Mandy? No, no, no, no, no. You can't do that sweetie. Do you have any idea what that would mean?

MARISSA: I know but . . .

ALEX: It would mean that Mandy and I would be over. Do you really want that?

MARISSA: Well, actually . . .

ALEX: Of course, you don't; neither do I.

MARISSA: You don't?

ALEX: No, why else would I go out with her?

MARISSA: I don't know.

ALEX: That's OK, don't worry about it. Let's just forget you said that.

MARISSA: But, you don't get it. I . . .

ALEX: Don't want to hook up again? I understand. It was totally fun though. If I wasn't with Mandy, you'd probably have to watch out for me.

MARISSA: (Nervously laughs.) Somehow I doubt that.

MANDY: Hey, is that Marissa? What is she doing over there with Alex?

JULIE: Oh, apparently they're friends. When you went to meet Alex the other night she came over and we — uh — we talked about them being friends.

MANDY: Really? Is that so? I think I'm gonna go over there.

JULIE: Are you sure you want to do that?

MANDY: Why wouldn't I? He's my boyfriend, and she's my friend.

MARISSA: No, you don't understand. What I was trying to say was . . .

MANDY: Hey, guys! How's it going over here?

ALEX: Oh, hey sweetie, um, we were just talking . . . about you . . . weren't we Marissa?

MARISSA: Right, that's what we were talking about. You two look so good together.

MANDY: I know, right? I didn't know you two were friends.

MARISSA: Oh, really? Well, we've been friends for a while.

ALEX: A long while. Long before you and I met. And you don't have to worry. Nothing has ever happened between us.

MARISSA: Yeah, nothing, over the years, has ever happened.

MANDY: Oh, that's nice, but I wasn't trying to hound you guys. I just wanted to see what was up.

(Julie enters onto the lighted side of the stage.)

JULIE: So, Marissa, did you decide about that thing?

MANDY: What thing?

MARISSA: Oh, nothing that concerns you, really.

MANDY: I know that, but . . .

MARISSA: I did decide, though.

JULIE: What are you gonna do?

MARISSA: Well, *(Speaking lower, close to Julie so no one else can hear.)* I was trying to tell him now . . . Then I was going to see what his response was and go from there. But now that there's suddenly a party over here with Mandy, I can't really say anything.

JULIE: Oh, I know what you're saying. I'll try to distract her long enough for you to talk to him

MARISSA: Thanks, that means a lot.

MANDY: Oh, come on you guys, don't keep secrets, that's not very nice. What were you guys talking about?

JULIE: Oh, um, I want to tell you, but not in front of the boy. Now, if we just go over there, I can tell you.

MANDY: What can be so secret Alex can't hear? *(Julie drags her away.)* I'll be back. *(They move to the side but not off stage.)*

MARISSA: So, Alex, we're alone again.

ALEX: That was a close one. Jeez, she's so annoying.

MARISSA: Then why go out with her! *(Consistently louder.)* If you can't stand her and you don't like to talk about her or be with her or do stuff with her, why be with her? Huh?

ALEX: Well, I — *(Noticing that Mandy can hear her.)*

MARISSA: We've always been so close. Why not me, huh? We had a good time this weekend, didn't we?

ALEX: Marissa, I don't think you should say that so loud. People *(Meaning Mandy.)* can hear you.

MARISSA: I don't care who hears; they'll find out anyway. *(Beat.)* I can't help it, Alex, I really care about you. I can't keep it in any longer. It's just that, since you've been going out with Mandy, I thought it would be easier to let you go and know that I have no chance. But it's harder. I know that you guys are together, and that's the way it is, but when we're together, I feel like . . . it works, you know? I can't help it. *(Beat.)* You . . . you don't even like her; it's all some crazy scam you have to get in her pants, and we all know it. But, I feel like it would be different with us. Saturday, that was so — relieving for me, because I felt that for the first time you might feel the same way I do at the same time I do. But, I guess it was just another stupid trick to get with a girl. I can't believe I was that stupid to fall for you. I don't even know why I did. What the hell is so special about you? You're not that great! Just . . . don't even try to answer. *(She tries to exit, but Alex gets up and stops her.)*

ALEX: No, that's not it at all. *(Softer.)* I just don't think we should talk about this here and now. I do like you, but I like her too; I'm with her. I can't explain it, but if you would just . . .

MARISSA: Save it for Mandy 'cause I don't want to hear it.
(Marissa runs off stage. Alex tries to catch up to Marissa, but Mandy steps in front of him, preventing him from getting off stage. She is obviously angry.)

JULIE: Wait, Marissa! *(Exits.)*

MANDY: So, is this true? You like her, too. You're with me to get into my pants? You don't even like me? What the hell is wrong with you, Alex! I thought we had something. *(Attempts to exit the other side of the stage, but Alex stops her.)*

ALEX: No, none of that is true. I don't even know what Marissa was talking about.

MANDY: Shut up. And what did you do that was so "relieving" on Saturday? Apparently before we got together that night. What, did you guys hook up?

ALEX: No, not at all, she's making way to big of a deal out of this, I can't help that she likes me . . .

MANDY: Answer my question Alex, enough with your babbling.

ALEX: We just kissed, OK. For a while.

MANDY: *Just* kissed? How could you do this to me? We're supposed to be going out.

ALEX: We are. I . . .

MANDY: What, just got bored of me?

ALEX: No, not really. I . . . I don't know why I did it. I'm sorry. Just forgive me, OK? We can start over, you know.

MANDY: Yeah, right. Just start over. I can't do that, Alex.

ALEX: Please. I'm begging you just . . .

MANDY: How about this, you leave me alone and I — I'll just leave you alone.
(Jerks herself away from Alex who is holding her shoulders and exits.)

SCENE 4

Stage left is the park bench, yet again, where Alex and Mandy met the other night. Stage right is Julie's bedroom. Marissa and Julie are together in Julie's room and are talking to Mandy over her cell phone. Mandy is at the park waiting for Alex to arrive.

JULIE: Now, Mandy, promise you'll listen to Marissa. She really is sorry.

MANDY: *(Alone sitting on the bench on the cell phone.)* I don't know if I can accept her apology. What she did . . .

JULIE: I know, I know. But it's not like she did it on purpose, it's not like she did it to hurt you. It's Alex you should be mad at. Alex is the one who did something unforgivable. And yet, there you are, waiting for him so he can apologize. Just hear her out, OK?

MANDY: Fine.

JULIE: Thank you. Here's Marissa.

MANDY: OK, what is it? I promised I would meet Alex here so we could formally break up. So, make it quick.

MARISSA: I'm so sorry you had to find out that way. Really I am but . . .

MANDY: But? There should be no buts in this apology.

MARISSA: But, I can't say that what I said wasn't true. About Alex I mean. I really did like him.

MANDY: Did? It sounded to me like those feelings were very alive last week in the cafeteria.

MARISSA: Yeah, then they were, but I've been thinking over the last couple of days, and I don't even know why I liked him anymore. I talked to him though, and we decided to no longer be friends.

MANDY: Really? I'm glad to hear that. It's a good start, but I don't know if I can go back to how it was before. You really hurt me, you know?

MARISSA: I know. I'm sorry. But we don't have to go back to the way it was before; we can . . . have a different friendship than before. Just . . . don't hate me, OK?

MANDY: Oh, Marissa, it's not you I hate . . . *(Alex enters and Mandy directs this toward him.)* It's you I hate.

MARISSA: What?

MANDY: Oh, he just got here. I have to go now. I have some unfinished business to get out of the way. But, don't worry about it. I forgive you, for now. We'll just have to talk later in person.

MARISSA: OK, bye. *(They hang up their phones.)* Well, she says she forgives me. I think lying about not liking him anymore helped. That was good advice.

JULIE: Yeah, I don't think she needs to know everything, especially after what happened last week. Maybe later you can tell her about . . .

MARISSA: About my new boyfriend.

JULIE: Right.

MARISSA: Well, I got to go, I'm meeting up with Alex later. *(Gets up and goes to leave.)*

JULIE: *(Struggling to say the words that get blurted out.)* Do you really think that it's a good idea? To even go out with him?

MARISSA: I know how it seems, but we talked for so long about it, and we were able to work it out. I can't help the way I feel, and knowing that he feels the same way, it's such an amazing feeling.

JULIE: OK, suit yourself.

END OF PLAY

DAYS GONE BY

7M

By Billy Van Dorn
Santa Margarita Catholic High School
Rancho Santa Margarita, California

Characters
ROBERT
JAMES
CHIP
DALE

Setting
First scene, Scene 4, and Epilogue take place in a park; Scenes 2 and 3 take place in a living room. The play begins in the present, goes back five years in Scene 2, and then progresses forward in time, returning to the first scene.

DAYS GONE BY

Prologue

Lights up on an empty stage. Robert enters alone spotlighted.

ROBERT: *(To the audience.)* Remember the days when it was just you and your pals? Before girls, before money, and before ego? Where did those days go? The wind didn't just blow them away. Some masked thief didn't snatch them in the middle of the night. I know what happened: Girls, money, and ego happened!
(Lights out.)

Scene 1

Lights up on a park scene. A small building with drinking fountains is lit by a flickering yellow light. James and Robert, seventeen to eighteen years old, enter. Robert is tall and lean; James is shorter and more stocky. They continue an earlier conversation.

JAMES: Wait . . . dried plums? Old people eat those, dumbass!
ROBERT: No they don't . . . that's prunes.
JAMES: Oh, shut up . . . so what else happened during this fun-filled night of hide-n-seek?
ROBERT: Well, Taylor tripped over a bike and didn't want to play in the dark anymore. At least not with the lights off. Chip and Dale showed up about fifteen minutes later stoned as a couple of martyrs, so I split before they knew I was there.
JAMES: Hold up a sec. *(James stops for a drink.)*
ROBERT: Damn, it's freezing out.

JAMES: Pansy. Suck it up.

(Two larger boys, Chip and Dale, enter. Chip enters in front of Robert and James; Dale enters from behind.)

CHIP: Hey guys. How's it goin'?

JAMES: *(Stepping forward.)* Chip, long time no see. Now, what do you want?

(James and Robert are unaware of Dale's presence.)

CHIP: Nothing, just passing through.

ROBERT: How's Taylor doing? I heard he fell at the skate park.

CHIP: He's fine. I hear your little antidrug club is starting to make quite an impact.

JAMES: *(Blocking Chip from Robert.)* Yeah, what's it to you?

DALE: They're my customers! *(Dale pounces forward in an attempt to sucker punch James, but is intercepted by a blow to the stomach by Robert. Everything freezes and Robert steps out to the audience once again.)*

ROBERT: Before things get a little too crazy, let me explain. My name is Robert. Robbie to my friends. This is James. He and I have been best friends since fourth grade. He's the two-time state wrestling champ, the next Hendrix on the guitar, and a recovering alcoholic. The big oaf on the left is Chip. Chip, James, and me were inseparable from fourth to eighth grade. Then Chip bulked up for football, not naturally, and became a user and dealer for Dale over there. For some reason, I became Chip's favorite punching bag halfway through freshman year. As long as James wasn't around to kick his ass. The big guy here . . . *(Jokingly puts his arm around the frozen Dale.)* is my buddy Dale. He's the bad ass of C.F. Montgomery High School. Don't be fooled by my moment of braveness . . . nobody messes with him. Nobody. I heard he put a kid in the hospital for a week just because the kid made eye contact with him. Now, before we get back to this dramatic standoff, let me jump back to the beginning.

(Lights out.)

Scene 2

Lights up on a living room with toys scattered about. Three boys, thirteen years old, come running in with backpacks and fast-food bags.

YOUNG CHIP: Let's hurry up and eat so we can go to Hal's before it gets too dark.

YOUNG JAMES: Yeah, easy for you to say, fat ass. All you do is eat.

YOUNG ROBERT: He's not fat, James, he just has ample layering for warmth.

YOUNG CHIP: Oh yeah, you guys are a riot! Let's pick on the fat kid again.

YOUNG ROBERT: Well, yeah! What else are you good for?

YOUNG CHIP: Shut up, Gumby, or do you want your mom to hear about your run-in with Deputy Tafoya?

YOUNG JAMES: Oh, that's cold Chip. Real cold. You knew he didn't do anything wrong.

YOUNG CHIP: Yeah . . . but I know we have seen birds fly. Have you James?

(Chip and Robert fall on the floor laughing. Robert enters as the action freezes.)

ROBERT: The portly fellow was Chip, before Pop Warner. Yes, we made fun of him, but we all made fun of each other. I was tall for my age . . . tall and lanky. So, naturally I was known as Gumby. The bird thing? Well, that was James's first pick-up attempt. He got so nervous all he could think to say was, "Have you ever seen birds fly?" *(Chuckles.)* Not one of his brightest moments. Now my dirty little secret from my mother . . . well it was nothing big now that I think about it. But I got caught stealing. I was caught with my pockets full of candy, but Chip and James ran home to get the money as the cops were pulling up. They totally had my back. Back then anyway.

(Lights out.)

Lights up on the same living room, minus the toys. The three boys enter in the middle of a "purple nurple" fight—trying to pinch each other's nipples. A phone rings. Chip answers.

CHIP: *(In an Asian accent.)* Pang's Kitchen. No MSG. Would you like to try our roast dog? I mean duck? Oh, uh, hold on a sec . . . *(He walks away to continue the call.)*

ROBERT and JAMES: Dale.

ROBERT: I heard he was expelled from his last school and that if his family didn't move, he'd be thrown in jail.

JAMES: Really? I heard gossip was for girls and gays!

ROBERT: Hey, what time is it?

JAMES: It's four-fifteen, why?

ROBERT: It's Tuesday! We have class, remember? We get to use the staffs today.

JAMES: Screw the staffs; just give me the swords.

(Chip gets off the phone.)

CHIP: What's goin' on?

ROBERT: I was just telling James here what a tiger your sister is in the sack. *(Chip charges Robert, but gets flipped over onto his back.)* I'm telling you, Chip, she's more of a freak than your mom is. *(He helps him up.)* Come to kung fu with us. Just this once. Ya never know, you may be better at it than you are at football.

CHIP: No, thanks. That Sefu guy creeps me out with those big, bulging, penetrating eyes. Besides, that stuff won't get me a scholarship.

JAMES: We're gonna be freshmen, and you're worried about scholarships? That's bull. You just don't want to go near the flower shop.

CHIP: Why would that stop me? I didn't do anything wrong.

JAMES: I know, but you can't tell me you have homework, otherwise you wouldn't be going to football.

ROBERT: Chip, that guy doesn't even work at the flower shop. He got fired for hitting you.

CHIP: I DON'T CARE ABOUT THE STUPID FIGHT!

ROBERT: Calm down, we believe you. Besides, he wouldn't mess with us again after the beating we gave him. *(Motioning to himself and James.)*

CHIP: What? I thought I told you guys to drop it! I'm going to practice. *(He exits.)*

(Lights dim as Robert steps out to address the audience.)

ROBERT: I wish this is where time could stop, or at least change. Chip was accused of sleeping with the flower shop guy's girlfriend. So when he went into the shop to pick up a corsage, words were exchanged, and Chip was outnumbered three to one. James and I didn't let that fly, so we met the flower shop guy at his car to help him change some flats, if ya know what I mean? *(Pounds his fist.)* Chip didn't remain the ivy league–bound jock we thought he would become. First, the studies dropped for football, but when he didn't make first string, he turned to steroids. He needed money for the roids, so he began dealing for Dale. Soon he quit football. He found the drugs to be more profitable. James quit kung fu to focus on his "studies." He really began focusing on his plethora of girlfriends. He is trying to find out if he is the father of one girl's baby. Me? Well, I have never been able to do anything alone, so I dropped kung fu. I didn't have any other talents, so I tried wrestling and hockey, but I was better at acting. I took up drama and started an antidrug awareness program at my school. Now, before I show you what happens, let me show you the last time the three of us were together.

Lights up on the park scene where the play began. Robert waits alone on a bench.

ROBERT: I'm sick of freakin' waiting for everyone. This is bull-shit. They don't care anymore. *(James and Chip enter from the opposite side of the stage.)* Well, it looks like they decided to waste their time on me after all.

JAMES: Hey, sorry we're late. I didn't want to leave Cheryl unfinished. *(Chip laughs and slaps him on the stomach.)*

ROBERT: Yeah, she is pretty demanding. Well, since you two fags got here so late, we don't have time to climb the trails.

CHIP: Why? Mommy wants you home before dark?

ROBERT: Just because your mom doesn't care enough to be home before three A.M., or post bail for you like we do, doesn't mean you need to take it out on me.

JAMES: Hey, so anybody see Jenna today? She decided to go for the pink thong. It must be Tuesday.

ROBERT: Shut up, James.

CHIP: Wow, you mean you actually do have some sense in that gigantic head?

ROBERT: Yeah, it even put me in classes with the rest of the sophomores! I hope you don't stain yourself in those little freshman classes. Again.

JAMES: Guys, seriously, cut it out. This is stupid.

CHIP and ROBERT: Shut up!

ROBERT: Don't tell him what to do, Juicer.

CHIP: What are you gonna do about it, drama fag?

(Robert takes a stance to welcome Chip's attack.)

CHIP: Screw it. I'm going to get something to eat. *(He exits.)*

ROBERT: What a bitch.

JAMES: Dude, what was that?

ROBERT: Nothing. He's an idiot, that's all.

(Lights dim as Robert steps out, spotlighted.)

ROBERT: Yeah, that was the last time we all "hung out." James didn't know Chip had jumped me a couple of times, nor did he know that he really was a juicer. But I couldn't tell him that. Chip and James were friends until the end of sophomore year, that's when James found out about the drugs and the beatings. James and I have grown apart; we see each other maybe every couple of months. But man, when we are together, it's as if nothing has changed . . . except the hole in the conversations where Chip should be. *(Lights out.)*

EPILOGUE

Lights up on the original scene where the play first started with Robert, James, Chip, and Dale.

ROBERT: Let's just skip to where we left off. *(Robert steps back into position.)* How's Taylor doing? I heard he fell at the skate park.

CHIP: He's fine. I hear your little antidrug club is starting to make quite an impact.

JAMES: *(Blocking Chip from Robert.)* Yeah . . . what's it to you?

DALE: They're my customers!

(Dale pounces forward in an attempt to sucker punch James, but is intercepted by a blow to the stomach by Robert. Chip flips out a knife and lunges at James, but James knocks the knife away and slugs him across the face, knocking Chip to the ground. Dale recovers and knocks James unconscious and grabs Robert from behind.)

DALE: Get your ass up and do it, Chip!

CHIP: I . . . I . . .

DALE: I swear, if you don't, I will. And you and your family will be next.

CHIP: Shut up. I'll do it. *(Chip hesitantly approaches with the knife.)*

ROBERT: C'mon Chip . . . think about it.

DALE: You shut your mouth. It's cost me enough business. He won't listen to you anyway. Do it, Chip.

(James begins to stir and sees what is happening.)

JAMES: Chip! What the hell are you doing?

CHIP: Shut up!

JAMES: Think about what you're doing, man . . .

CHIP: I said, shut up!

DALE: C'mon! I'm not gonna wait any longer!

(Dale pushes Robert into Chip as James tackles Robert out of the way colliding into Chip. Dale runs offstage. Robert stands up and nudges James, but he does not respond.)

ROBERT: James! James! C'mon man, this isn't funny! *(Chip stirs and Robert grabs him and pulls him up.)* Your mother . . .

CHIP: Wait! Please, Robbie, please . . .

(The two boys hold each other, crying as the lights fade out.)

END OF PLAY

CATHY AND JOEY STEINBERG'S BIG NEW YORK ADVENTURE

6M, 5F

By Amanda Marzo
Aliso Niguel High School
Aliso Viejo, California

Characters

NEWS REPORTER: Ambitious female.

CATHY STEINBERG: Flamboyant, dramatic; dresses with great flair. She wears sunglasses to disguise herself.

JOEY STEINBERG: A young man dressed as a small boy.

MR. MARK MARX: A high-strung, flamboyant theater director; always wears black.

STAGEHANDS: Three to five extras (no lines) to mill around onstage for Scene 2.

JUDY: Mark's assistant; also always wears black.

RONALD: Stagehand.

MAHEBE MAHOMED: Taxi driver, box office attendant.

BLANCHE: Character from *A Streetcar Named Desire*.

AUDIENCE MEMBER: Male or female.

USHER: Male or female.

STEVEN SPIELBERG

Setting

Because of the diverse locations that occur in this play, it is suggested that you keep the sets as simple as possible. Specific locations can be denoted by a single piece of furniture or by lighting.

CATHY AND JOEY STEINBERG'S BIG NEW YORK ADVENTURE

Prologue: The News

We see a woman News Reporter behind a desk holding up a disturbing picture of a woman in a very inappropriate position with what appears to be an older man.

NEWS REPORTER: We interrupt this program to bring you breaking news. Earlier today, Steven Spielberg's wife, Kate Capshaw, filed for divorce, when she caught her husband in bed with another woman. Other reports today have quoted Spielberg as saying that "it was an affair to remember." The sexual excursion has caused him to take a vow of celibacy, and he has sworn off filmmaking forever. If I may quote, "I've found the sexual encounter with Ms. Cathy Steinberg to be so orgasmic that not even making art films will suffice." One thing seems to be on everyone's mind in Hollywood today: "Where is Cathy Steinberg?"

Scene 1

An alleyway behind the theater. An older woman, Cathy Steinberg, enters stage left. She wears sunglasses and a bandanna over her messy hair. She carries a huge purse and has on high heels. She is very fast paced, looking as though she is in a hurry. She takes out a piece of paper from her purse and looks up and down at the paper.

CATHY: *(She speaks in an unnaturally strong Jewish accent.)* Well, this seems to be the place. Joey! Get out of the cab! We're late! Joey!

(Joey, a young man who is dressed and acts like a young boy, enters, skipping from stage left holding a lollipop in one hand and a bottle of glue in the other.)

CATHY: I've said it once; I'll say it a hundred times, "Don't talk to the taxi drivers." They're angry, dirty immigrants who don't understand a word you're saying. *(She looks at the items in his hands.)* Where in the heck did you get those?

JOEY: I found it in the taxi!

CATHY: Give me those! *(Grabs the two items and places them in her coat pocket. She starts to fuss over him.)* Now, do you remember the lines Mommy taught you?

(Joey turns away and puts his head down and starts to cry.)

CATHY: *(Her hand on his back.)* Oh, don't cry, don't cry, baby. It'll make your eyes red, and then what will we do? *(He looks at her sadly. Pause. He starts crying again. She takes out a hanky, wipes his face, and puts it to his nose.)* Blow! *(Joey blows his nose, and Cathy puts the hanky back in her purse.)* Oh, I hate this place just as much as you do! *(Turning to him arms spread out.)* But we have nowhere else to go . . .

(Joey looks up at Cathy with big, round, pleading eyes. Sniffs.) No! I already told you . . . we can't go back to Hollywood. *(Joey looks at Cathy angrily. Guilty conscience.)* Because Mommy did Mr. Spielberg a tiny favor that Mrs. Spielberg didn't agree with, and so now Mommy has been shunned from that cheap, unforgiving town that was once her home. *(Angry.)* So we had to come here, to New York, to make a new start. *(Joey looks sad.)* It's all right! Just think of it as an adventure . . . like Indiana Jones . . . *(Cathy starts to sob; she drops to her knees.)* Oh, Steven. Our love was too strong for this world. But one day, one day, we shall be together, and our love will no longer be shunned, but shall be praised around the world as a love that can't be broken . . . *(Sobbing.)* . . . I shall never love again. *(Cathy puts her head down crying hysterically. Joey backs away, too terrified to go near her. He slowly creeps toward her and puts his hand on her back. He goes to her purse and*

takes out the hanky and hands it to her. She grabs the hanky and blows into it. Joey pats her on the back comfortingly.) Thank you. *(Stands up.)* I'll show them! I'll show them all! I don't need them! I don't need anyone! *(Joey looks sad. Cathy goes to him, hand on his back.)* Oh, except you, sweetie. We're gonna be the biggest team since Garland and Minnelli. We'll be bigger then . . . then . . . Bernadette. We'll be bigger than Lloyd Webber or . . . or . . . Sondheim. Our name will be too big to put in lights. They'll need to make special lights just for us. I can see the headlines now! BROADWAY'S GREATEST DUO: CATHY STEINBERG AND HER SON, JOEY! *(Joey claps his hands with excitement.)* Now, did you practice your lines like I told you to? *(Joey nods happily.)*

Good. Now I know you have never done a stage show before, but we'll just keep that to ourselves, won't we? For all that Mr. Marx knows, you've been doing theater your whole life. Now don't worry, acting on stage is just like acting on television . . . just without cameras. And if you forget your lines, sneeze. That way I can read your lines to you from offstage, and no one will ever notice. Now, I'll be sitting in the audience watching you, so if you forget your lines, what do you do? *(Joey sneezes.)* That's my boy! Now, fix your hair, honey! I want you to look your best for Mr. Marx before we go in. *(Fixes his clothes.)* There, that's better! OK, well we'd better go in; the show's about to start. Come on.

SCENE 2

Backstage. They enter backstage stage left, and there is a frenzy of excited energy of an opening night. People are getting dressed and moving sets and props. There is much talking and nervous laughter. A man, Mr. Mark Marx, in a black outfit, wearing a headset and holding a brown clipboard, can be seen pacing back and forth.

MARK: Five minutes, people!

CATHY: Hello! Mark? My name is Cathy . . . uh . . . Catherine . . . uh . . . Oh-Oherra . . . Igins. Catherine O'Higgins. We spoke on the phone.

MARK: Oh, thank Oprah you're finally here. I was so nervous that you wouldn't make it. Is this Joey?

CATHY: In the flesh . . . *(Pushes Joey forward, fixing him up more.)*

MARK: Oh, good! Judy! Judy! Will you get Joey here to the dressing room and see if you can find him a costume? Thanks. *(A woman, Judy, dressed in black and wearing glasses, exits with Joey. Cathy follows Joey as he exits, fixing his hair. Joey looks annoyed.)*

CATHY: Wow! Such excitement! I haven't seen anything this chaotic since closing night of *Evita* when Pattie LuPone blew out her voice. *(She laughs.).*
(Ronald enters stage right holding a prop and crosses to stage left.)

MARK: *(To Ronald.)* Ronald, don't put that there! It goes stage right, not stage left! *(Ronald looks annoyed and sighs.)* Don't give me that attitude right now! I can't handle it. *(To Cathy.)* I am so sorry for the short notice, but the boy who plays our "young man" was sadly crushed by one of our set pieces this morning during rehearsal.

CATHY: Oh, the poor thing. And how long will he be "unavailable?

MARK: Well, until he gets out of his coma, there's really no way of knowing.

CATHY: What a shame. *(Under her breath.)* Yay!

MARK: I'm sorry, what was that?

CATHY: Oh, nothing! I was just saying that you've got nothing to worry about because Joey has performed in *A Streetcar Named Desire* many times as the "young man." Why, he was in a revival with Marlon Brando himself, just the other day in fact.

MARK: *(Looks excited and interested.)* Marlon Brando, huh? I never knew he was in a revival of *Streetcar*. Well, that must have been right before he passed away. It must have been very hard for you to see him so recently, and then hear he had passed away so suddenly.

CATHY: Oh, yes! Most shocking!

(Mark stares at Cathy curiously for a few seconds.)

MARK: Hey, haven't I seen you before?

CATHY: *(Panicking, covering face with scarf.)* Oh, I don't think so! I just have one of those faces.

MARK: No! I'm sure I've seen you somewhere! Do you know Stephen? *(Cathy gasps.)* Stephen Sondheim?

CATHY: *(Relieved.)* Oh, no! Perhaps you saw me in an Off-Broadway production of *My Fair Lady?*

MARK: No, that's not it. Huh . . . how strange. I could have sworn I've seen you somewhere before.

CATHY: Well, New York is a big place. Maybe you bumped into me somewhere.

MARK: No, that's impossible . . . I've sadly never seen the sunlight of the outside world . . .

CATHY: Well, I'd better be going. The show is about to begin, and you're a busy man.

MARK: Good-bye Ms. O'Higgins. I'll make sure to watch after Joey for ya.

CATHY: Oh, and by the way, before I forget, there's one tiny little thing I forgot to mention. Joey has allergies up the wazoo; he's practically allergic to everything. So be careful what you feed him. He's especially allergic to perfumes, grass, cat hair, dog hair, spaghetti, lettuce, hair spray, and a whole load of other stuff I'm not really sure how to pronounce . . .

(Joey enters in knickers and a hat with a plaid shirt.)

CATHY: Well, hello gorgeous! Look at you. Oh, don't you look absolutely adorable! Come here and give Mommy a kiss. *(Joey pecks Cathy on the cheek.)* Now, you be a good boy for Mr. Marx. Mommy's going to be in the audience. Remember . . . *(Whispering.)* . . . what do you do if you forget your lines? *(Joey sneezes. Cathy pinches his cheek.)* That's my boy.

MARK: *(Offering a box of candy.)* Joey? Would you like a chocolate?

(Joey crosses to Marx, nods, smiles, and opens his mouth.)

CATHY: No! You can't!

MARK: Why not?

CATHY: *(Grabs chocolate and puts it in her coat.)* Because of his condition.

MARK: *(Concerned.)* Oh! He's allergic to chocolate?

CATHY: No! He's just terribly obese!

(Cathy exits with the box of chocolates. Mark and Joey watch her leave, looking confused.)

SCENE 3

Outside at the box office for A Streetcar Named Desire. *Cathy enters. An Arab man is selling tickets behind the booth. When he sees Cathy standing in line, he starts to laugh evilly.*

CATHY: What's so funny?

MAHEBE: Oh, nothing . . . nothing. Would you like to buy a ticket, ma'am?

CATHY: Well, actually, I was hoping to get in free. You see my son is in the play.

MAHEBE: Oh, really? How wonderful! That will be sixty dollars.

CATHY: Whoa! Wait a minute! Did you just say sixty dollars?

MAHEBE: Well, unless you want orchestra seating. In that case, it would be a hundred dollars.

CATHY: A hundred! You've got to be kidding me. That's insane. That's more than my son makes per show.

MAHEBE: Yes, well tough cookie sister, OK? Now, are you going to buy a ticket or not? You're holding up the line.

CATHY: *(Sweetly.)* Listen. *(Laughing.)* What is it going to take to get you to give me a free ticket?

MAHEBE: *(Laughing.)* You don't remember me, do you?

CATHY: Should I?

MAHEBE: *(Stops laughing.)* Oh. You New York women are all alike. So self-centered, so rude, so racist. Well, even if you don't know who I am, I know who you are . . . Cathy Steinberg!

(Cathy holds her hand over her heart and gasps.)

CATHY: What gave it away? The hair or the boobs?

MAHEBE: You were the rude woman in the taxi!

CATHY: Oh . . . oh! The taxi driver!

MAHEBE: *(Laughing.)* "Don't talk to the taxi drivers, they're angry, dirty immigrants, who don't understand a word you're saying." You ignorant woman! Not so high and mighty now, are you? I understood everything you said!

CATHY: But why are you working here? I thought you were a taxi driver.

MAHEBE: I took a second job, working in the box office for extra money.

CATHY: Oh. How's that going for you?

MAHEBE: It's pretty good. I don't have to work that late, and I get free tickets to the shows. Just the other day I saw *Thoroughly Modern Millie*. That Sutton Foster is a real peach. But none of that matters because I'm not going to sell you a ticket!

CATHY: Oh, please! My son is in the show, and if I don't get in, the show will be ruined!

MAHEBE: Should have thought of that before you called me a filthy immigrant! Cathy Steinberg! *(He picks up the phone to call someone.)*

CATHY: Hey! Who are you calling?

MAHEBE: The *New York Times*. I'm sure they would be very happy to know YOUR whereabouts. I'm sure I'll get good money for it, too.

CATHY: Wait a minute! Put down that phone! Put it down! Please! I'll do anything. Anything! Just put it down! Please!
(*Mahebe puts down the phone smiling.*)
MAHEBE: Anything?
CATHY: Anything!
(*Mahebe laughs.*)

SCENE 4

The play A Streetcar Named Desire *is being performed on-stage. Blanche sinks faintly back in her chair with her drink. She is fanning herself with a palm-leaf fan.*

BLANCHE: Ah me, ah me, ah me . . .
(*Her eyes fall shut and the fan drops from her fingers. She slaps her hand on the chair a couple of times. Joey comes along the street sneezing uncontrollably and rings the bell. Cathy is sitting in the audience. She stands up clapping and cheering.*)
CATHY: Yay! Joey! That's my boy up there! That's my boy!
(*Audience Member looks annoyed, so Cathy sits down.*)
AUDIENCE MEMBER: Hey, haven't I seen you somewhere before?
CATHY: No! Of course not. Now shut up and watch the play.
BLANCHE: Come in.
(*Joey takes a double take at the audience and opens his mouth in horror. He becomes completely still, frightened out of his mind. Blanche regards him with interest.*)
BLANCHE: Well, well . . . what can I do for *you*?
(*Joey stands there frozen, looking at the audience.*)
BLANCHE: I said . . . what can I do for YOU? (*Joey remains completely still, saying nothing. Blanche laughs nervously. She grabs Joey's face and turns it to hers.*) WHAT CAN I DO FOR YOU?!
(*Joey sneezes in Blanche's face. Blanche, with calm hatred,*

wipes off her face with her hands. Cathy stands up and runs to the stage.)

CATHY: *(Whispering to Joey.)* I'm collecting for *The Evening Star.* *(Joey looks down at his mother and smiles. Cathy runs back to her seat and sits down.)*

JOEY: I'm collecting for *The Evening Star.*

BLANCHE: *(Annoyed.)* I didn't know that stars took up collections.

JOEY: It's the . . . the . . . the . . . *(Sneezes.)*

CATHY: Paper!

JOEY: Paper!

BLANCHE: *(Confused.)* I know, I was joking . . . feebly. Will you have a drink?

JOEY: Oh, yes please!

(Joey runs over to the bar and pours himself a drink into a small glass. He quickly takes a gulp and spits it out.)

JOEY: *(Shocked.)* That was *alcohol*!

BLANCHE: *(Really confused.)* Yes! Oh, well, now let's see . . . No, I don't have a dime! I'm not the lady of the house. I'm her sister from Mississippi. I'm one of those poor relations you've heard about.

(Joey sneezes.)

CATHY: *(Yelling to the stage.)* That's all right. I'll drop by later!

USHER: Excuse me, ma'am. You're being too loud. I'm afraid I'm going to have to ask you to leave.

CATHY: Oh, so sorry. I'll keep it down.

USHER: No, ma'am. You're going to have to come with me.

CATHY: Oh, come on! My son is onstage right now. If I leave, he'll be devastated!

(The Usher grabs Cathy by the arm and pulls her out of her seat.)

CATHY: How dare you! Unhand me at once! I'll have you know I paid good money for this ticket. *(They exit.)*

JOEY: That's all right. I'll drop by later. *(He starts to go out. Blanche approaches.)*

BLANCHE: Hey! *(Joey turns back shyly. She puts a cigarette in a long holder.)* Could you give me a light? *(She crosses toward him. They meet at the door between the two rooms. Joey sneezes. There's no reply. Joey sneezes again. There is still no reply. Joey starts to panic.)* DO YOU HAVE A LIGHT? *(Joey looks around and spots a lamp sitting on a small table. He reaches for it and hands it to her. Blanche laughs nervously.)*

BLANCHE: No, you silly boy. A light for my cigarette.

JOEY: Oh.

(Joey searches through his pockets and finds a lighter and holds it up. He tries to light her cigarette, but he doesn't know how.)

BLANCHE: *(Angrily.)* Temperamental, is it? Here, let me try. *(Blanche grabs the lighter from Joey and lights the cigarette.)* There. *(He starts away again.)* Hey! *(He turns, uncertain. She gets closer to him.)* Uh . . . what time is it?

JOEY: *(Looking down at his watch.)* It's about ten-fifteen, why?

BLANCHE: *(Frustrated.)* So late? Don't you just love these long rainy afternoons in new Orleans? . . . *(She touches his shoulder. Joey giggles nervously.)* You . . . uh . . . .you didn't get wet in the rain?

JOEY: *(Nervously.)* No . . . no . . . no . . . no.

BLANCHE: Did you step inside a drugstore? Did you have a soda?

JOEY: No. Mom said I couldn't have a soda on account of my obesity.

BLANCHE: *(Trying to stay in character.)* Oh . . . but . . . but . . . you're not obese; you're a beautiful young man! Has anyone ever told you that you look like a young prince out of the Arabian Nights?

(Joey laughs uncomfortably and stands like a bashful kid. Blanche speaks softly to him.)

BLANCHE: Well you do honey lamb! Come here. I want to kiss you, just once. Softly and sweetly on your mouth. *(As Blanche moves in to kiss Joey, he backs away and laughs nervously. Blanche attempts to kiss him another time, but*

Joey backs away a second time.) Like I said, I want to kiss you, just once, softly and sweetly on your mouth!

JOEY: *(Running away.)* Ahhh! Get away from me crazy lady! *(Joey starts running around the stage through set pieces and knocking down props as he goes. Blanche angrily chases after him.)*

BLANCHE: You are going to kiss me and you are going to like it!

JOEY: Ahhh!

BLANCHE: Get over here! *(As Joey runs around, he accidentally trips over the rug and falls to the ground. Blanche catches up to him and crawls on top of him and grabs his face.)* I want to kiss you. Just once. Softly and slowly on your mouth! *(Blanche kisses Joey. There is a pause after the kiss. Joey smiles at Blanche. Blanche looks horrified.)*

JOEY: Wowy-wow-wow!

(Blanche screams. Just as Joey kisses Blanche, Cathy enters buttoning her shirt and fixing her hair.)

CATHY: *(Angry.)* Ahhh! Get your hands off my baby!

(Joey and Blanche look up at Cathy horrified.)

JOEY: No, Mommy, don't. I love her!

BLANCHE: What are you doing? Get off the stage!

CATHY: No one touches my boy and lives!

BLANCHE: Yes, but it's part of the play! You're ruining the play!

(Cathy punches Blanche in the mouth. Blanche stumbles to the bar. Blanche takes a glass and pours a drink and throws it into Cathy's face.)

CATHY: Ahhh! My eyes! I can't see.

(Blanche punches Cathy in the face. Cathy grabs Blanche's scarf and starts to choke her with it.)

JOEY: Two women that I love are fighting over me. What should I do? *(Joey goes down into the audience. To audience member.)* Scoot over. *(Joey sits down in the audience to watch the fight. Mr. Marx enters along with the Usher.)*

MARK: *(Pointing to Cathy.)* That's her. That's the one who ruined my play! Get her!

(Blanche takes a tray and tries to bash it onto Cathy's head. She misses and hits the Usher on the head instead. Cathy drops her glasses and drops to the floor to look for them. Mark chases after her. Mark is standing behind her when something drops on his foot causing him to moan in pain. There is a large gasp from the audience. Cathy puts on her glasses. Everyone is silent and staring at her. She looks around, and to her surprise the entire audience recognizes her. Mahebe enters.)

MAHEBE: CATHY STEINBERG! *(Laughs.)* Ladies and gentlemen! Boys and girls! This horrible woman who stands before you is none other than that gold-digging movie- and play-ruining CATHY STEINBERG! Oh, yes! You've all seen her on the news. Don't let the wig and the sunglasses fool you. It is she!

AUDIENCE MEMBER: *(Standing up.)* I knew I recognized you! You're the girl that slept with Steven Spielberg! *(There is a loud uproar from the audience. Cathy looks around helpless and trapped. The audience yells angrily. Cathy waves her hands frantically.)*

CATHY: Wait! Wait! Wait! Everyone stop! I know what you're all thinking. I know you're angry. Yes, I slept with Steven Spielberg. I admit it. I'm not proud of the things I did. My bad decisions . . . but he was so . . . so . . . nice! We were drunk, we were hot, we clicked. It was the heat of the moment, you know? We couldn't fight the feelings we had for each other. What can I say? I was in Hollywood, down on my luck. I couldn't get any work. I had a son to feed. I almost . . . I almost took up . . . I almost took up stripping! *(Sobbing.)* Until one day, I met a man. He took me in, gave me food and shelter. It wasn't just hot, spur-of-the-moment sex; it wasn't just a one-night stand. No people! It was love. But, I was kicked out of Hollywood for it. Forever condemned to walk the streets of America alone. The only thing I had to live for was my son. So do you blame me for coming here and trying to find work? Do you blame me for trying to give my son a good life? I only hope you can find it in your hearts to forgive a poor, old, sorry woman like me.

SPIELBERG: CATHY STEINBERG! *(Steven Spielberg runs out from the audience to the stage where Cathy is.)* I've been searching everywhere for you! And by God, you are just as beautiful as ever. Why did you leave me, Cathy? That night was so passionate and hot . . . and when I woke up, you were gone! You are the one! I can't believe I could even survive before you came along. Once I had you, nothing else mattered to me anymore. I hadn't lived until that night! And every day, I die a little bit more without you. But here you are! In a theater. When you should be in my bed!

CATHY: Steven!

SPIELBERG: Cathy, my love! *(They embrace.)* Why did you leave me, Cathy? Why?

CATHY: Our love wasn't meant to be Steven! You have a wife. I have a son. You're a famous director. I'm a working mother. You're rich. And I'm middle class. *(She starts to cry.)* That's why I had to leave.

SPIELBERG: My dear. Don't you know that nothing, not even a wife, can stop love? Nothing could ever tear us apart. Did Indiana Jones give up when the Nazis captured the girl he loved? Did Dr. Grant run away when raptors were going to eat his wife? Did Tom Hanks give up on saving Private Ryan? Did Forest Gump forget Jenny after all those many years? Never! Cathy! You are the girl I was meant to be with. And I would climb every mountain . . . go through booby-trapped temples and travel through time just to be with you! I've spent every last cent of my money searching for you. And I love you! So won't you do me the honor of being my wife? *(He goes on his knees and places a ring on Cathy's finger. Slowly, one by one, the audience members stand up and start to applaud.)*

CATHY: What? What was that you just said?

SPIELBERG: Be my wife!

CATHY: No . . . no . . . before that.

SPIELBERG: I love you!

CATHY: *(Shakes head.)* No . . . before that!

SPIELBERG: I've spent every last cent of my money searching for you?

CATHY: *(Nods.)* That's what I thought you said. Hey, what's that over there? *(The audience and Spielberg turn their heads to see what she's pointing at. Cathy grabs Joey.)*.

SPIELBERG: I don't see anything!

CATHY: Keep looking.

(She tries to grab Joey, but Joey clings to Blanche. Cathy urges Joey to come with her. Joey looks sadly at Blanche and gives her a big kiss. Cathy and Joey exit. The lights fade as the audience and Spielberg are still searching for what Cathy was pointing to.)

EPILOGUE

Inside an airplane.

CATHY: England! I love the British. They're so polite and cute. So they have bad teeth . . . so what?

JOEY: But Mommy, why did we leave America when the people in the audience forgave us?

CATHY: Because eventually they would have hated us for something else. And you know New York . . . they don't quickly forget people like us.

JOEY: But what about Mr. Spielberg? He wanted to marry you. I would have had a new daddy!

CATHY: Fathers are overrated dear . . . all anyone ever really needs is their mother. And you have the best mother in the world. Don't forget that!

JOEY: *(He rolls his eyes.)* England? Oh . . . Mommy does this mean we have to change our accents again?

CATHY: Yes. Yes it does.

JOEY: Do we have to?

CATHY: Yes.

JOEY: OK. *(English accent.)* So Mumsy, what kind of crazy adventures do you think we're in for next?

CATHY: I don't know, son. I just don't know. One can only guess . . .

JOEY: Maybe when we get there we can have a nice spot of tea.

CATHY: Jolly good. Jolly good.

(The lights fade on them laughing.)

END OF PLAY

CONCEALED

1M, 1F

By David Galanter
Laguna Beach High School
Laguna Beach, California

Characters

IAN: Seventeen-year-old high school senior. A questionable character because of his inability to take anything seriously or give any helpful input in a situation; very sarcastic and almost never fails to come up with a degrading remark or sexual innuendo toward Kira,

KIRA: A sixteen-year-old high school junior. Also sarcastic, but unlike Ian, she has limits; doesn't mind just playing along with Ian's comments, but sometimes he goes too far or just won't shut up,

Setting

Ian's living room during the school year. There is a seat stage right facing stage left and a couch slightly up stage left of it facing down stage with a coffee table center stage. There is also a small magazine table down stage left with a few *Electronic Gaming Monthly* (EGM) magazines on it. Off stage right is the front door; off stage left is the kitchen.

CONCEALED

Lights up. Ian is lying down on his couch reading EGM, when someone starts knocking on the door. Ian gets up and goes off stage right.)

IAN: *(Off stage.)* Glad you could make it.

KIRA: Really?

IAN: Nah.

KIRA: Screw you.

IAN: You know you want to. *(They walk onstage.)*
(Kira has a folder and a schoolbook under her arm. In the first few lines, Kira goes and sits down in a chair and opens her book and folder on the coffee table.)

KIRA: Where are your parents?

IAN: Out.

KIRA: How exotic. *(Kira notices Ian's lack of school supplies.)* Where's your homework?

IAN: It's in my backpack. *(Pointing behind him, not showing a lot of concern.)* Hungry?

KIRA: Not really. Why?

IAN: Hungry girls get me off.

KIRA: What? . . .

IAN: So we can eat!

KIRA: Well, I don't know! You're hungry?

IAN: Starving.

KIRA: Grab something to snack on.

IAN: Nah, I'll eat later. *(Ian goes back to reading his EGM.)*

KIRA: Whatever. *(Kira looks at Ian for a moment as he's reading his magazine.)* I thought you wanted to study.

IAN: Yeah, my mood changed.

KIRA: Lucky me. *(Kira pulls some things out of her binder.)* Hey, you left this at school during lunch. *(Kira pulls out a single piece of paper. It looks like a worksheet.)*

(Ian bends his magazine away from his face for a second to look.)

IAN: Huh, how 'bout that. *(Goes back to his reading.)*

KIRA: *(Finding this typical.)* Are you planning on doing it?

IAN: Ya know, I hadn't planned on it.

KIRA: I see. *(Puts down the paper.)* How's your GPA doin'?

IAN: Fine, thank you, how's yours?

KIRA: *(She smiles a bit.)* You are such a bastard. *(Gets homework out from her binder to work on. Sighs.)* I hate chemistry.

IAN: Sorry.

KIRA: Thanks for the help.

IAN: As if I'd even be able to help you.

KIRA: You're a year ahead of me.

IAN: That doesn't mean anything. *(Blaming her for it.)* You take too many AP classes.

KIRA: I'm sure you could find a way to make yourself useful.

IAN: And I have. *(Smiling big with his magazine in hands. A moment passes. Some nervousness in his voice.)* Hey, did you ever find out if you have to work later tonight?

KIRA: Yeah, Kaylee's gonna work tonight so I don't have to go in.

IAN: Cool, so, what do you wanna do?

KIRA: Well, Ian . . . I'd like to finish this. *(Referring to her homework.)*

IAN: OK, after that, what do you wanna do?

KIRA: I dunno, you wanted to go somewhere?

IAN: That's the idea.

KIRA: Like?

IAN: Movies.

(Kira gives him a look of annoyance.)

IAN: What?

KIRA: No.

IAN: Why not?

KIRA: Because, I refuse.

IAN: Ouch.

KIRA: Ian, I have a boyfriend, and I would never date you.

IAN: Oh I see, friends with benefits.

(Kira rolls her eyes and just goes back to her work.)

IAN: I get it. *(Sighs.)* Well, Kira, you drive a hard bargain. I'll think about it and get back to you when the time is right.

KIRA: What time is it?

IAN: Not yet. I'm not done making my decision.

KIRA: Just give me the time asshole.

IAN: Eight forty-seven.

KIRA: Aw, frick.

IAN: What?

KIRA: I just remembered, I was supposed to call Jason at eight-thirty. *(Kira tries to grab for the phone. Ian teases her for a second and slips the phone down the front of his pants.)*

IAN: What do you see in that guy anyway?

KIRA: *(Shocked and disgusted.)* Well, he's not a douche bag.

IAN: Eh . . . there's just something about him I don't like.

KIRA: Oh, what's that? He gets some from me? *(She makes an attempt to get the phone, but Ian swerves around her.)*

IAN: Jeez! I haven't tried to grab your ass for like four days. *(Grabs her to make her stop.)* Hey! I don't trust him.

KIRA: Well, that's you.

IAN: Plus, he's kind of boring.

KIRA: He is not.

IAN: Come on, we both know the guy couldn't entertain another human being if his life depended on it.

KIRA: That is so not true. *(Laughing a bit.)*

IAN: Yes it is. *(Pulls out her cell phone and gives it back.)* You know it is. You need somebody more fun and exciting.

KIRA: *(Picking up one of his gaming magazines.)* Oh, what like you?

IAN: *(Backs off a bit.)* Yes.

KIRA: Oh, yeah, I bet you're a real thrill. *(She moves his magazines to sit down.)*

IAN: Shut up. Hey, you ever read these? They're interesting.

KIRA: I'm sure.

IAN: Well, if I'm so boring, how come you didn't just go to Jason's house to do homework?

KIRA: Just because I'm going out with him doesn't mean I can't still hang out with other friends, too, numb nuts.

IAN: I know but I'm just SOOO boring.

(Kira's next few lines are very emotionless. She starts to dial Jason's number on her cell phone while she talks.)

KIRA: *(Sighs.)* You're not boring.

IAN: *(Being difficult.)* You think so.

KIRA: I do not.

IAN: No, you said I was boring.

KIRA: I did not.

IAN: You implied it.

KIRA: I'm very sorry.

IAN: No, I can't forgive you. Not after that.

(Jason picks up.)

KIRA: *(On phone.)* Hey hon! . . . What's up? . . . Yeah? . . . *(Chuckles a bit.)* Nooo . . . Heh, I'm sure . . . Oh . . . Yeah, you want to? . . . OK . . . Cool, yeah, whenever you're ready . . . All right . . . Bye!

IAN: What was that all about?

KIRA: Jason just got off of work. He's gonna pick me up in a little bit.

IAN: I thought we were gonna hang out.

KIRA: Yeah, well I thought we were gonna study, so I guess we're even. *(Gives a little evil smile.)*

IAN: *(Admitting defeat.)* Oooh. All right. Touché.

(Kira goes back to her studies.)

IAN: You're still going to work? I thought he was gonna be here in, like, two seconds.

KIRA: Ya know, I have a lot of work to do, and this is not helping me finish this any faster.

IAN: I know, I'm just wondering what you could possibly be working on that wouldn't just be worth putting it away for the last few minutes you're here.

KIRA: Do I have a reason why I wouldn't want to get this out of the way now?

IAN: Me. *(Smiling annoyingly.)*

KIRA: You're not even paying attention. You're reading your crap.

IAN: I can put it down. We can do something.

KIRA: I don't even want to know what your idea of doing something is.

IAN: You like it.

KIRA: You wish.

(Feeling defeated, Ian walks away and sits down to continue reading in one of his magazines.)

KIRA: *(As soon as Ian sits down.)* I'm thirsty. Is there anything in your fridge? *(Knowing he'd have to get up for her.)*

IAN: Yeah. *(Ian gets up, then pauses, and smiles big.)* Let me *not* get that for you. *(He sits back down.)*

(Kira gets up and heads toward the kitchen.)

IAN: You do exactly as I say.

(Kira stops for a minute annoyed but then moves on toward the kitchen.)

IAN: You wanna get me something too, while you're in there? *(Ian slaps Kira on the ass as she walks by him. Kira turns around looking at him like she's had enough.)*

IAN: *(As if he's talking to a five-year-old.)* Come on. You can do it. Get Ian a drink.

(Kira turns around completely and starts heading back the other direction toward Ian.)

IAN: Awww, the kitchen is the other w . . .

(Kira pulls Ian in toward her and kisses him. As the kiss is happening, Ian isn't kissing very well: his arms are to his sides and his eyes are wide open. Kira, on the other hand, has her arms around him and doesn't seem nervous.)

KIRA: *(She stops kissing him, and he's frozen stiff. Talking as if she's speaking to a five-year-old.)* What was that? I'm sorry, that was rude. You were saying something? Oh, you were finished? Are you sure?

(Ian attempts to answer back coolly but just ends up stuttering.)

KIRA: What? I can't hear you. What was that? Huh? Yeah, that's what I thought.

(Kira then leaves the room to get her drink with a big smile that she challenged his image. Right when she leaves, Ian does a frustrated movement to himself, angry that he broke down and lost his cool. He sits himself down in the chair and starts fiddling with Kira's notebook. He flips the cover to see what's on the front. Kira enters.)

KIRA: Curious are we?

IAN: *(A little nervous in his speech now.)* I guess. How come you have pictures of babies on your binder?

KIRA: Because, I love little kids; they're adorable.

IAN: Not ALL little kids.

KIRA: Yes they are! *(Chuckling.)*

IAN: What about that one? Do you think that one's cute?

KIRA: *(Still laughing.)* Of course!

IAN: Really?

KIRA: Yes.

IAN: I dunno . . . It looks like he's kinda got a drooling thing going on. You like that?

KIRA: He's a baby! And yes, it's adorable.

IAN: You think so?

KIRA: Yes.

IAN: Yeah, me too.

KIRA: *(Doubtful.)* . . . Really?

IAN: Am I not allowed to think that children are cute too?
(Kira leans back in her chair looking at Ian in suspicion.)

IAN: What?

KIRA: I know what you're trying to do.

IAN: What?

KIRA: You're trying to be all Mr. Sensitive because you think you have a chance to woo me since I kissed you.

IAN: *(Slight pause.)* No.

KIRA: Ian, I kissed you to prove a point.

IAN: Which was?

KIRA: You're all talk. You're always trying to act all cool and apathetic, but the minute you actually have to walk the walk . . . you freeze up. It just proves that you are not the annoying, sarcastic person who you try to be all the time. It's just an act to pick up girls or be cool, which I might add doesn't work very well in both cases, and I called you on it. Nothing more.

IAN: So, you admit that I could be Mr. Sensitive.

KIRA: *(Angry.)* No, that I still doubt.

IAN: You don't know for sure then.

KIRA: Well, it's hard to tell with you. I'm not exactly sure who you truly are.

IAN: So then how do you know what I really felt when you kissed me?

KIRA: OK, fine, what did you really feel, Ian? *(Kira's cell phone starts ringing. On the phone.)* Hey! . . . . Oh, really? . . . OK . . . See ya soon. Bye.

IAN: What is it?

KIRA: Traffic sucks, he'll be a little longer.

IAN: I see . . . You think tube head would mind that you kissed me?

KIRA: I knew I was going to regret that.

IAN: No, for real . . . You don't think he'd care?

KIRA: I didn't cheat on him. It's not like I was giving away affection behind his back.

IAN: No? *(Kind of getting back to being cocky.)*

KIRA: *(Looks at Ian annoyed.)* No.

IAN: OK.

KIRA: *(Sighs.)* Sometimes this whole facade of yours is entertaining, but other times it pisses me off that I can't just talk to you seriously.

IAN: I'm sorry.

KIRA: *(Aggravated.)* Don't be . . . just . . . stop.

IAN: I didn't think I bothered you so much.

KIRA: You don't, but right now I'd like for you to stop. Would it kill you just to show yourself for five minutes?

IAN: No.

KIRA: Then, why don't you?

IAN: I am.

KIRA: Yeah?

IAN: Yes, this is me.

KIRA: Are you ready to talk like a grown-up?

IAN: You want me to work with you or not?

KIRA: OK, OK, so you promise to answer honestly?

IAN: Yes!

KIRA: Wow, I can't believe I'm actually the one annoying you.

IAN: Congratulations.

KIRA: Thank you. All right, all right. Ummm . . . hmmm . . . something good . . . Oh! Do you think that attitude helps you get girls?

IAN: Why?

KIRA: Because it seems like you think it does.

IAN: Maybe.

KIRA: When was the last time you kissed a girl?

IAN: Do your homework.

KIRA: Come on!

(Ian starts to pick up another EGM.)

KIRA: No, no, no. *(She takes it out of his hands and tosses it out of reach.)* Is it really that difficult? Come on.

IAN: *(Sighs.)* Three minutes ago.

KIRA: Before that smart ass.

(Ian just stares at her with a blank expression.)

KIRA: No way . . . Serious?

IAN: Do your work.

KIRA: Never? Awww, man . . . Now I feel bad. I kinda ruined that moment for you.

IAN: Trust me. It's fine.

(Kira gives him a little hit on his shoulder.)

IAN: Ow! What was that for?

KIRA: For coming on to me.

IAN: How was that coming on to you? Since when have you cared about that?

KIRA: Always. I just never hit you. You said it all pervy.

IAN: No . . . Maybe I meant that it was fine as in I don't care because I never get anything like that anyway. Oooh see? Now what was that for?

KIRA: Being pathetically cute, I guess.

IAN: *(He smiles a bit nervously.)* I need a drink. *(He gets up and heads toward the kitchen.)*

KIRA: Who do you have a crush on?
(Ian stops and turns around.)

IAN: What makes you think I have a crush on anyone?

KIRA: I know you do.

IAN: *(Ian looks at her a little annoyed.)* I figured so much.

KIRA: Well?

IAN: Don't.

KIRA: What?

IAN: I know you can guess.

KIRA: I do too; I just want to hear you say it.

IAN: Why?

KIRA: Because you shouldn't be so ashamed to admit what you're really like and what you really want.

IAN: What's the problem? You laugh, you often don't care, and I'm not the only one who makes smart-ass remarks, mind you.

KIRA: Yes, but at least I have limits. I can do that, but I also know when to be serious. I'm not a mystery; people know who I am. I know there's more to you then this. You know I don't actually believe the bad-ass Ian is honestly interested in Nintendo power.

IAN: EGM.

KIRA: Whatever.

IAN: *(Defensive.)* They're two different things.

KIRA: OK.
(Short pause.)

IAN: I'm not a mystery. People know who I am, and they know me as this, because this is me.

KIRA: No, it isn't. I can tell. Under everything, you've always been, like . . . there's something completely different . . . and it disappoints me sometimes. I wish you could just show who you really are, just for a second. Prove to me there's more to you then this. I'm giving you an opportunity here. *(Ian neglects to respond.)*

KIRA: Ian, please?

IAN: What opportunity? Nobody would like me the way you think I am, the way I really am.

KIRA: *(Pause.)* I might.
(Ian turns his head to focus on her intently. A car horn honks outside. Kira gets all her stuff together.)

KIRA: I guess I'll see you later.

IAN: *(Reluctant.)* Good-bye.
(Kira turns around slowly and exits. Ian is left alone, obviously upset with himself. Kira re-enters. Ian turns around to face her, happy at first. She walks to the coffee table and picks up something of hers.)

KIRA: Forgot my calculator.

IAN: *(Disappointed again.)* Yeah, you would.
(Kira sinks her head down disappointed and starts to walk toward the door. Ian turns away from her as she is about to leave again.)

IAN: It was you.
(Kira stops as she is an inch away from being gone and turns slightly back toward Ian's direction.)

IAN: It was always you.
(She is torn. They both remain still for a moment. She exits. Ian stands for a moment in pain, thinking he just showed himself, and for nothing. He sits down on the magazine table staring blankly at the floor. He picks up one of his magazines and flips through it briefly, then slams it down in frustration. Kira enters.)

IAN: What happened? Where's Jason?

KIRA: He's gone, and I'm betting he's not going to want to come back for a little while.

IAN: What did you say to him?

KIRA: Let's just say I told him I needed someone a little more fun and exciting.

IAN: Oooh, I see. *(Sounding cocky.)* So . . .

KIRA: Eh-eh . . . stop. Now, you were doing well.

IAN: You sure you're going to be able to deal with me being such an asshole?

KIRA: We'll work on it.

IAN: *(Sexually.)* What does that mean?

KIRA: Shut up asshole, you know what I want.

(Ian smiles genuinely. He stops in front of her, nervous for a moment. Kira takes his arms and puts them around her waist. The music starts to fade in as she puts her arms around his neck. They move in smiling and experience their first true kiss. Slow blackout.)

END OF PLAY

BITE ME

2M, 8F (2M Voiceovers)

*By Samantha Brewer, Lori Boucher, Liz Council,
Brittany Davila, Olwen Friesen, Dani Hamilton,
Samantha Hochhalter, Emily Jorgenson, Cody Levin,
Elsa Richardson, and Adele Young*
Trollwood Performing Arts School
Fargo, North Dakota

Characters
MALE VOICEOVER 1
MALE VOICEOVER 2
BURT
SVETLANA
URSULA
CHRISTINA
BLAIR
IRIS
CHARLIE
ISABEL
KELLEN
JORG

Setting
The arm of a young boy.

*Note: All the characters except for Burt are mosquitoes; Burt
is a tick. Voiceovers are humans.*

BITE ME

At rise, in blackout, we hear Voiceover 1 and Voiceover 2. Voiceover 2 should be the voice of a young boy.

VOICEOVER 1: Hey, kiddo, should we set up our stuff here?

VOICEOVER 2: Yeah . . . this is a really cool spot . . . right by the river!

(Lights up. We see a bar or what appears to be a bar. Burt is busy setting up behind the bar. He is whistling while he works. Svetlana enters frightened and disoriented. She moves to the bar where she immediately takes out a long red straw, pierces it into the bar itself, and begins sucking up the liquid as fast as possible.)

BURT: Hey now, little lady . . . slow down, why don't ya? There's plenty to go around. This stuff is very rich . . . you need to pace yourself.

SVETLANA: Must . . . drink . . . haven't had food . . . for . . . days and days . . . *(She continues to drink voraciously.)*

(Ursula enters, also disheveled and seemingly disoriented.)

URSULA: Whoa, baby . . . what is this place? Where the heck am I?

SVETLANA: Must . . . drink . . . more . . . more . . .

BURT: *(To Ursula.)* Hey, friend, this here is Burt's Bar. Finest selection around. Sweetest wine of our time. What can I do you for?

URSULA: Sweet wine? Yes! That's exactly what I need. I've been feeling a bit woozy lately . . . something's going on out there.

BURT: Yes, I know. I've had a hard time finding a decent location to set up. But this place is working out just fine. Had quite a bit myself, earlier today. *(Burt pats his very full stomach.)*

URSULA: Yeah, I can see you have. I definitely need some of that. *(Burt takes a long red straw and thrusts it into the bar.)*

BURT: There you go . . . drink up!

URSULA: Thanks! *(She begins sucking up the liquid.)*

(Christina and Blair enter. Christina keeps spinning around in circles. Blair is clearly trying to help her.)

BLAIR: Well . . . they're at it again. The mist is thicker than ever. Can't see a thing. Can't find any food. It's making everyone feel discombobulated. Especially this one — she won't stop dancing, and I don't understand what she's talking about!

CHRISTINA: *(Flitting about the bar; she speaks with an Italian accent.)* He loves me . . . he loves me . . .

BLAIR: Who loves you? Who?

CHRISTINA: *(With a silly little grin.)* He loves me!

BLAIR: I give up. She's bonkers.

BURT: *(Leading Christina to the bar.)* C'mere hon. Have a little nourishment. This is gonna make you feel much better. I guarantee it.

BLAIR: Set me up, too, Burt. I'm starving.

(All three move to the bar. Burt thrusts straws into the bar for Blair and Christina, and they begin to drink. Iris enters. She gazes about the bar almost as if in a hypnotic trance. Blair notices her entrance.)

BLAIR: Iris? Did you get caught in it? Are you OK? Iris?

IRIS: *(Twirling around in circles.)* Isn't the world *fantastic*? Utterly, supremely, incredibly . . . FANTASTIC!

URSULA: Well, she's obviously been out there way too long.

BLAIR: Obviously. Her mind is gone. How can she possibly think the world is fantastic? Not for our kind anyway.

URSULA: It's not that bad.

BLAIR: Oh really? *(She sighs.)* Sometimes I really wish I were a bird or something.

URSULA: A bird? Oh brother.

(Charlie enters in a flurry, calling for Iris.)

CHARLIE: *(Looking around.)* IRIS! Are you here? Oh, please be here . . . Iris? Hey . . . have any of you seen . . . *(Sees Iris twirling about.)* IRIS! Oh, my God! What have those slobs done to you—my poor Iris. My poor little sister. That mist . . . those . . . what do you call them again? People! Those people! Putting that fog upon us as if we were nothing but mere irrelevant little creatures! We have feelings too! We deserve to live our meaningful two-week existence just as much as anyone else. How dare they do this to my Iris! Look at her! Just look at her! I wish I were a vegetarian like my brother. If all of us were vegetarians, things like this would never happen.

IRIS: *(Very mellow.)* I'm fine, Charlie . . . I'm completely at peace—I feel so significant. I understand my place in the world. I feel phenomenaltastic!

CHARLIE: No, honey . . . that's the poison talking. It makes you feel like you're going crazy, but you're not really going crazy, it just makes you feel like you're going crazy, and then you wind up going crazy!

SVETLANA: *(Still drinking at the bar.)* Must . . . drink . . . must get nourishment for my babies . . . must . . .

URSULA: Whoa, baby, save some for the rest of us, would you?

BURT: *(Moving Svetlana away from her straw for a moment.)* I told you dear . . . there's plenty to go around. This food source you're feeding off of is supplying all of you with this delicious and nutritious beverage. This feeding station just happens to be a healthy, red-meat eating, candy-bar snacking All-American Boy! I found him this morning . . . just latched on to the little guy's pant leg and climbed on up.

BLAIR: You always find the best, Burt.

BURT: Thanks. I do what I can!

CHRISTINA: *(Looking up from her straw and speaking to no one in particular.)* He loves me . . . he loves me!

BLAIR: Yeah, yeah . . . sure he does. *(To the others.)* Just humor her.

(All characters come up to the bar and begin sucking up the liquid. Burt remains busy facilitating them. Isabel enters carrying a giant M&M. She is trying to nibble on it. She is unsuccessful.)

ISABEL: Hey, Burt — take a look at this!

BURT: What the hell is that?

ISABEL: I dunno. I'm trying to eat it though. Can't seem to find much to eat these days. We might as well try this, don't you think?

SVETLANA: *(Continuing to drink.)* Must eat . . .

CHARLIE: Is it food? Is it safe? Is it . . . vegetarian?

ISABEL: I dunno. I'm pretty sure it's food. It's hard to crack this thing open — and there's no sticky liquid in the middle — just this brown stuff — kinda sweet — hard to drink.

IRIS: *(Approaching Isabel and touching the M&M.)* Wow . . . this is awesometastic! A new food source!

BLAIR: This is no food source! *(She kicks the M&M.)* This is . . . junk!

ISABEL: *(Still nibbling.)* Well . . . it kind of tastes good. You're always so negative, Blair.

BLAIR: I'm a realist. And the reality is . . . we cannot survive on whatever *this* is!

(Isabel shrugs and continues to nibble away on the M&M. Kellen enters, running and screaming.)

KELLEN: *(Out of breath.)* OK . . . you guys are not going to believe what just happened to me! There I was trapped in its web . . . moving toward me, almost on top of me . . . I saw its jaws. My entire life flashed before my eyes — every single thing that happened to me last week. I knew it was the end.

ISABEL: And then what happened?

KELLEN: It started acting very strange. It started slowing down — its head drooped, its web became loose, and I managed to escape. A narrow escape, but an escape nonetheless. I'm free. I won! I have triumphed over our worst enemy. I beat the SPIDER!

CHARLIE: It wasn't you! You didn't do anything. That spider probably got poisoned too. Didn't you notice all the fog outside? Didn't you notice that you can't find any food anywhere? The hosts are rejecting us! It's the end of the world, and you're acting like a superhero!

KELLEN: Well . . . I feel like a superhero. That spider almost ate me!

CHARLIE: Well, if the spider didn't get you . . . the mist will. Or you'll starve to death. Either way . . . it's the end.

BLAIR: It's the end all right.

BURT: Calm down, everyone . . . This host is being very hospitable. We have plenty of food for everyone. Come and have a drink to soothe your nerves.

BLAIR: Easy for you to say, Burt. Nothing affects you.

(Jorg enters wearing a Hawaiian shirt, straw hat, and lei. He is sipping pomegranate juice from a coconut shell.

JORG: Dudes . . . how's it hangin'?

BURT: Jorg, what are you doing here? You don't drink.

BLAIR: Well, he's drinking something.

ISABEL: And it's red . . .

CHARLIE: And it smells sweet . . .

IRIS: It looks unbelievably supertastic!

SVETLANA: *(Moving toward Jorg and his drink.)* Must have food . . . must drink . . . *(She snatches the drink out of Jorg's hand.)*

JORG: *(Annoyed.)* Ka-frickin' boom, babe — that was just *rude*!

SVETLANA: Must drink for my babies . . . *(She starts to suck up the liquid. She takes a sip and then spits it out.)* Aaahhh . . . I have botulism!

CHARLIE: You've poisoned her! What did you give her to drink?

JORG: I didn't give her anything to drink. She grabbed it out of my hand. She's very pushy. You females always get so crazy when it starts getting misty outside.

CHARLIE: They're poisoning us out there, and now you're poisoning her in here.

JORG: Chill, dude. It's not poison. It's totally healthy. Natural. That's all I ever drink. It's the lovely red nectar from a pomegranate. It totally sustains me through my day.

CHARLIE: And just what do you do all day that requires sustaining?

JORG: Well, babe, I've got this great pond of stagnant water out back where I do all my best work . . . if you know what I mean. Care to join me?

BLAIR: Are you out of your mind? They're putting stuff in that pond — they're putting stuff everywhere. Soon you won't be able to find any decent nectar anywhere. You'll start going crazy, too, just wait and see. There's no where to go except here. But we're not going to be able to stay here forever — eventually this feeding station will close its doors for good.

ISABEL: And that's why I think we should try eating this. *(Holding up the M&M.)* There's no place left to go. The mist is everywhere!

URSULA: I can't eat that crap. I have a very sensitive digestive system. It has to be this. *(Indicating red beverage.)* This and nothing else.

SVETLANA: Must . . . have . . . blood . . .

URSULA: Yes, we know. We all must have blood. Except for him. *(Points to Jorg.)*

CHARLIE: We could try to live like Jorg and become vegetarian. We can try surviving on pomegranate nectar.

JORG: It's a totally bitchin' way to live, let me tell ya.

SVETLANA: Babies . . . babies need blood. *(She returns to the bar and continues to drink.)*

URSULA: She's right. The babies need blood.
(Iris looks as though she is just about ready to exit the stage. Charlie sees her and pulls her back in.)

IRIS: Doesn't the air smell fantastic?

CHARLIE: Oh, Iris, you're so far gone. She went right through the thickest part of the fog before we made it in here. Look what it did to her.

IRIS: All the colors are so beautiful.

JORG: I don't know why you're so worried. She seems to be having a blast!

BLAIR: Christina too — she's really gone . . .

CHRISTINA: He loves me . . . Oh, how he loves me . . .

JORG: *(To Christina.)* Hell-lo Betty!

CHRISTINA: Ciao amore. Do you love me?

JORG: I do. I love ya babe. *(He moves toward Christina suggestively.)*

BLAIR: Hey you, pomegranate pupa—stay away from her! She's not ready for that kind of responsibility.

(Jorg moves away from Christina and toward Ursula.)

JORG: What about you, babe? Wanna check out my pond?

URSULA: Wanna check out my proboscis? Get away from me!

CHRISTINA: *(To Jorg.)* I love you.

BLAIR: Christina . . . don't . . .

URSULA: Oh, leave her alone. It's her time.

BLAIR: I think she's a little young. And he's definitely not the right male for her.

ISABEL: It's her choice. I was her age when I found love. Now I just love this . . . *(She continues to nibble on the M&M.)*

JORG: *(With complete insincerity.)* Well, I love you, too.

CHRISTINA: You see? He loves me . . . he loves me!

JORG: Yes, he does. Shall we go to the romantic shallow waters of my stagnant pool of love?

CHRISTINA: Mi amore.

(He offers Christina his arm. She takes it murmuring all the while "he loves me, he loves me." They exit.)

BLAIR: That guy makes me sick. Now he's gonna knock her up, and there won't be any food for her eggs. But do you think he cares? Not one bit.

URSULA: Well, at least he won't be around for very much longer. After she gets through with him, he'll be dead in a day.

BLAIR: Yeah, that's true. That's comforting.

URSULA: You're not that sleazy with your own kind of females, are you Burt?

BURT: Of course not . . . I have the utmost respect for you egg-layers. Why do you think I set up this fine establishment? To keep you ladies well nourished.

BLAIR: You're a true gentleman, Burt. A rare breed, I have to say.

KELLEN: Hey, everyone, I think we should band together and take advantage of the fact that this mist is weakening all those spiders out there. We can wipe them all if we work together. We'd never have to worry about them again! I think we can do it. What do you say?

CHARLIE: How can you possibly think of spiders at a time like this? That stuff is killing all of us, don't you realize that? All of us . . . spiders, flies, ticks . . .

BURT: With all due respect, Charlie, it's not really affecting us ticks!

CHARLIE: Well, it's taking its toll on the rest of us. Just take a look at my sister, why don't you? She's lost her mind!

KELLEN: Sorry . . . I didn't mean to upset you . . . I just thought . . .

CHARLIE: *(Interrupting.)* Well, I'm upset, OK! I mean, today is the last day of our lives . . . Isn't anyone else upset about that?

IRIS: *(Philosophically.)* Don't be upset Charlie. Don't you feel alive? I feel alive. ALIVE! Breathe in those fumes — they're nothing to be afraid of. They're intoxicating!

(A slight hissing sound is heard. Isabel drops her M&M with a gigantic thud. She looks around slowly and sniffs the air.)

ISABEL: It's closer. Do you smell it?

(Iris and Charlie speak simultaneously.)

IRIS: It's wonderful!

CHARLIE: It's awful!

BLAIR: *(Matter-of-fact.)* I guess this is it. This is the end. Man . . . I still had another week left in my life cycle, and I was gonna try to do some serious living! Oh well . . . nothin' we can do about it now, I guess.

KELLEN: I still think we could take those spiders. And if we die trying, well at least our kids would never have to worry about them.

SVETLANA: Babies . . . my babies . . . I can't leave my new batch of babies . . .

URSULA: There's three hundred of them. I think they'll be able to manage without you.

(All characters start to sway and bounce as if on a train.)

BURT: Uh-oh. I think we're on the move. Hold on ladies — looks like we're going for a ride.

(Ursula, Blair, Burt, Charlie, Kellen, and Isabel grab on tightly to the bar as they move and shake and jostle up and down. Svetlana continues to drink. Iris continues to dance.)

CHARLIE: Iris! Get over here! You're gonna to fall off. You're going to fall right off this boy's arm!

IRIS: *(Spreading her wings.)* I'm free — I'm F R E E E E E . . . *(Iris flies off. Sound cue of a loud slap.)*

CHARLIE: Oh, no . . . Iris—she's gone . . .

(We hear the more distinct sound of the hissing of an aerosol can.)

ISABEL: They're coming. I can hear it.

BLAIR: I can smell it.

SVETLANA: I can taste it.

KELLEN: We're goners.

URSULA: Hey, Burt, thanks for everything.

BURT: So long, ladies. It certainly has been my pleasure serving you.

(They all hunker down under the bar as a mist begins to cover the entire stage. The lights change, flicker, go dark, and when they come up, all the characters are dead with their legs straight up in the air. They are all slightly twitching. Burt is the only survivor. He starts to sweep up the corpses as he shakes his head.)

BURT: Damn! I hate when this happens. Now I have to start all over again. Oh, well . . .

(Burt exits. The lights begin to fade as we hear:)

VOICEOVER 1: So? Did you get 'em?

VOICEOVER 2: I can't believe it. Seven of them! That's some of kind of record, huh, Dad?

VOICEOVER 1: Thank goodness for that bug spray. I don't know what we'd do without it.

VOICEOVER 2: Wow! They sure do have some big mosquitoes here in Fargo.

VOICEOVER 1: Yup. They sure do.

END OF PLAY

FLYING TO THE SUNSET

1M, 1F

By Gloria Powell
West Potomac High School
Alexandria, Virginia

Characters

IAN: A troubled teen trying to escape his chaotic home life.
RACHEL: A childhood friend and neighbor of Ian. She has been a constant mediator of his problems and is in general a caring and understanding soul.

Setting

A sidewalk in a tired, poverty-stricken neighborhood. It's in the evening, during the fall.

FLYING TO THE SUNSET

Hostile yelling is heard off stage, and then stops abruptly. Ian enters quickly with a suitcase; he gets halfway across the stage when Rachel comes running after him.

RACHEL: Hey, Ian, Wait up!
  (He stops.)
IAN: You following me?
RACHEL: Maybe . . . I heard the screaming from my porch *(She eyes the suitcase he is carrying.)* What's that for?
IAN: What do you think? I'm leaving, Rachel. Getting away from here.
RACHEL: *(Sighs.)* I don't think I can count how many times I've heard you say that.
IAN: Yeah, well I'm not joking any more. I've had it here. Every day gets worse and worse . . .
RACHEL: Was it your dad? Did he hit you?
IAN: No, he wouldn't hit me. He has to beat on someone weaker than him.
RACHEL: So he hit your mom?
IAN: No! He didn't hit nobody.
RACHEL: Then what happened?
  (Pause. He puts down the suitcase and runs his fingers through his hair and over his temples.)
IAN: He doesn't want me here. He thinks I should leave. And you know what I think? I think maybe he's right. *(He kicks the suitcase.)* I hate it here! Day after day, I work my butt off, and for what? I'm just trying to live Rachel. I don't need people screaming at me because their life is screwed, you know?
RACHEL: Yeah.
IAN: Anyway, there's no reason to stay. No one wants me here.
RACHEL: That's not true. *I* want you here, and so does your mom.

IAN: My mom? Ha! She's ashamed of me!

RACHEL: She's not ashamed of you, Ian. *Jeez*! Why would you say something like that?

IAN: She hates the fact that she can't provide for me like she wants to . . . can't give me all the things she's dreamed of getting me.

RACHEL: She still loves you though; nothing will change that.

IAN: You know she wanted to be a singer? She was going to school for it, then she got pregnant with me and had to drop out. Now she hums these sad-sounding songs around the house, knowing her dream will never come true, and I'm the reason for it.

RACHEL: She doesn't blame you for that, Ian. Stop blaming yourself for everything you can't change! You just can't carry everyone's problems on your shoulders. Eventually, they'll fall, and you won't have changed a thing. *(She looks him straight in the eyes.)*

Your dad's a jerk. You know it, I know it . . . heck the whole neighborhood knows it! But guess what? It's not your fault. Yeah, your mom had you at a young age; she wishes things might have turned out differently, but so what? It's not your fault, Ian!

IAN: Thank you for the inspiration . . . but I'm still leaving.

RACHEL: *(Loudly.)* Yeah?!

IAN: *(Louder.)* Yeah!

RACHEL: *(Biting back frustration.)* Well, where you gonna go? West to California? That's what you told me last time.

IAN: No . . . I figured I might join the army

RACHEL: *The army*? The army, Ian? Great. Now I really know you've lost it.

IAN: I'm serious.

RACHEL: Yeah, that's why I'm afraid

IAN: I don't want to be a bum like my dad . . . I need to be someplace where I can make something of myself. You know, do something constructive.

RACHEL: Yeah, like blow up something? Real constructive, Ian. *(Overlapping.)*

IAN: What's it to you Rachel? Why should you care?

RACHEL: Because I'm your friend, that's why! *(Softly.)* I don't want to see you get hurt.

IAN: I'm already hurt! I've been hurt for a long time now.

RACHEL: I'm sorry, Ian.

IAN: It's not your fault. You care. I appreciate that. You've been there for me, you know? Listening to all my sap stories . . . always trying to make me feel better. God knows you have your own problems to deal with.

RACHEL: I don't mind, I never did.

IAN: You know as much as I've hated it here, you were the one that's always kept me from leaving.

RACHEL: Then don't go, Ian.

IAN: I don't see any other way.

RACHEL: You could stay with us! My mom wouldn't mind. And my uncle could get you a job at his shop . . . we'd work something out.

IAN: You'd do that for me?

RACHEL: You know I would.

IAN: Thanks, Rachel, but we both know that wouldn't work.

RACHEL: Yeah, I know . . . this . . . this really sucks.

(They stand quietly, both absorbed in their own thoughts. Ian clears his throat in an attempt to break the silence.)

IAN: Hey, do you remember that book you gave me for my birthday last year?

RACHEL: The poem collection you swore you'd never open? Of course.

IAN: I've been reading it lately.

RACHEL: *(She smiles skeptically.)* Really?

IAN: Yeah, there's this one that I kind of like. I don't know . . . it just kind of stuck with me . . . *(He paces around and looks to the sky before reciting.)* "One day I'll fly away from here. I'll grab my bag and head off into the sunset. The darkness will fade, the hurt, the pain, and disappointments will last no longer. I will whistle a happy tune and my wings will soar above the clouds where no one can stop me."

RACHEL: *(Overlapping softly.)* "One day I'll fly away from here. I know it is time. I won't look back. I will look forward and embrace all that I missed in my time of darkness. Then all will be right that should be, and I'll become the someone I dreamed I could be. I cannot fear because I know one day I'll fly away from here." *(Pause.)* It's one of my favorites.

IAN: It's time for me to fly away, Rachel.

(There is a pause, then they embrace.)

RACHEL: *(Close to tears.)* I don't want you to go.

(They gently break away.)

IAN: Well, I do. I'm ready.

RACHEL: Promise, promise, promise you'll write to me!

IAN: I don't really write letters . . .

RACHEL: Ian, *promise!*

IAN: *(Laughing.)* Yeah, I promise. *(He pulls her into a final hug.)* I'm going to miss you. *(Pause.)* It's not the end for me, Rachel. It's just the beginning. *(He playfully jabs her in the arm.)* I'll see you at the sunset.

(Ian picks up his suitcase, walks to the other end of the stage. He shares another knowing stare with Rachel before exiting. Rachel looks after him and pulls her jacket closer. The warmth that the encounter has brought is gone, and she quietly exits the stage.)

END OF PLAY

DEAR MOM

3F

By Stephanie Heckel
California High School
Whittier, California

Characters
RACHEL
MOM
CHILD/TEEN

Setting
Two scenes are played simultaneously: Rachel as a young woman writing at her desk in a college dormitory room and a series of episodes from her past as a child and teenager.

Note: One actor plays both Child and Teen.

DEAR MOM

On stage left there is a desk and chair. The lights are dim. A young woman walks onstage, puts her jacket on the back of the chair, and pulls the chair out from under the desk. She sits down, leans over, and turns on a desk lamp. At the same time, a spotlight circles her. She pulls out a pad of paper and a pen from the desk.

RACHEL: Dear Mom, College is great. My room is nice *(Pausing, she looks around and lets out a long sigh.)* and . . . I miss you. I've been thinking about you a lot. I wish we could talk, but I'm so busy, and well, I haven't really had the time. I've been thinking about all the good times and bad times we shared. Do you remember back when I was four? *(Now there are two people on stage right, one playing Mom. The other is playing Rachel as Child.)* How I would sing and dance and say . . . *(The younger Rachel starts to dance around and stops to wave at the crowd.).*

CHILD: Hi, there, Grandmas and Grandpas! *(Mom runs over and speaks to the crowd.)*

MOM: Sorry, she just loves people.

CHILD: Wait, wait . . . Mommy watch me. *(She twirls around in circles and starts to sing.)* "You are my sunshine, my only sunshine. You make me happy when skies are gray. You'll never know dear how much I love you . . ."

MOM: Sweetie, hold on there, you're going to run out of energy.

CHILD: Wait, let me finish the song . . . "So please don't take my sunshine away!" I can act too. Do you want to see? Or I can tell jokes.

CHILD and RACHEL: Or . . .

RACHEL: How about those times when you were proud of me, like when I first brought home a report card with straight A's. True, this was just the first of many to come. You and

Dad were so proud that me, you, Charlie, and Dad went out for some ice cream that very night. Oh, the good old days. My favorite family outing was every Fourth of July when the four of us would go to the park to see the fireworks at . . . *(Child turns around and lies down. Mom turns around.)*.

CHILD and RACHEL: night . . .

CHILD: time is here! Finally! The fireworks should be starting soon! Where are Charlie and Daddy? They're going to miss the fireworks.

MOM: Don't worry, your dad and brother went to get us all some pretzels from the snack bar. They'll be right back.

CHILD: Oh . . . Wow! Look, the fireworks are starting! Wow, they're so pretty!

MOM: *(Sitting down next to Child.)* Did you have fun today?

CHILD: *(In awe of the fireworks, she looks over at her mother.)* Yeah, this was the best birthday ever. *(Kisses Mom on the cheek.)*

MOM: Even though you're getting older, you'll always be my little girl.

RACHEL: Too bad I couldn't stay that way . . . just your little girl. Two years later, "I became a woman." I was so scared. I thought I was going to bleed to death. But then, you explained what was going on. I entered the eighth grade the following year. There I met Emily, and she and I quickly became good friends. When you first met her you said . . .

MOM: I like her. There is just something about her that's a little off. You said she got transferred. Why?

TEEN: *(Whiny.)* Mom, it's no big deal. She's cool, and she's my friend. You don't even know her.

MOM: Just look at the way she dresses in those punk rock clothes. I just want you to keep an eye on her.

TEEN: You said never judge a book by its cover! God, Mom!

RACHEL: But in some ways you were right. Emily did turn out to be a really bad influence in years to . . .

RACHEL and MOM: come . . .

MOM: . . . back here! I'm not done with you yet. *(Both come back onstage. Mom is mad.)*

TEEN: *(Tired like it's four in the morning.)* Please, Mom, I just want to go to bed. You yelled at me already in the car.

MOM: No! I told you I didn't want you going to that party. It started too late, and I didn't like the neighborhood. *(Teen starts to walk away.)* Wait just a minute! Do you know how it feels to come home to an empty house after work and realize that your daughter is missing? I was horrified!

TEEN: Mom, cool down. I'm fine. Get off it.

MOM: This is the last straw. I will not have you sneaking out of the house. I'm sorry, but you are not allowed to see Emily anymore.

TEEN: But, Mom, no! She wasn't . . .

MOM: Save it, Rachel. My mind is made up. Tell Emily to look elsewhere for friends.

TEEN: You don't know what you're talking about!

MOM: I know that she's the one that brought you to that party! I'm not stupid.

TEEN: But you can't tell me what to do. You don't run my life! I'll hang out with her, or anybody else, if I want to.

MOM: Please, I'm doing this for your own good. Trust me, she is a bad egg. You'll be happier without her around to bring you down. Sweetie, please! You have so much going for you, good grades and . . .

TEEN: What part of "you don't control me" don't you understand? She's my friend, and I trust her. I'm not going to do anything stupid.

MOM: What about tonight? Sneaking out was pretty stupid.

TEEN: Fine! Whatever. I won't see her any more, I promise.

RACHEL: But, sad to say, I didn't keep my promise to you. I still hung out with Emily, but I hid it from you, and I'm sorry I did. I got into some bad things. I even skipped school sometimes without you knowing, but reality came crashing down on me *(Starts to tear up.)* when Charlie got into his accident. After we lost him that November, I was so angry.

I thought I was angry at you, but really, I was angry at my-self for the fact that I didn't talk to Charlie as much as I should have. But then the worst thing that could have hap-pened was next. Dad . . .

RACHEL and TEEN: walked out on us.

(Mom is crying off stage.)

TEEN: How could you, Daddy? Why, why are you leaving? Please, Charlie just left us two months ago. We need you now more than ever, and you're leaving. Why?

MOM: I don't know what happened. We were a happy family . . . *(Mom tries to put her hand on Rachel's shoulder, but Rachel steps away.)*

TEEN: No, we weren't! It's your entire fault Dad left. You were the one that threw out all of Charlie's stuff because *(Mock-ingly.)* "you couldn't take it," and you know that you broke Dad's heart. You broke up this family. You're the one who screwed up our lives!

MOM: *(Crying.)* Rachel, please! I tried my best, really I did, but things just got out of hand. *(Teen shakes her head at Mom and leaves. Then Mom leans up against the window and cries out.)* We were happy! We were!

RACHEL: That's when things took a turn for the worst now that it was just you and me in the house and things were too quiet . . . *(Teen and Mom onstage — dead silent.)*

MOM: *(Long pause.)* So . . . how was school? *(Long pause.)* Are you . . . still going to that school dance of yours?

TEEN: *(Snaps.)* Like you care! *(Storms off.)*

RACHEL: And things went wrong.

(Both Mom and Teen come storming onstage. Teen has her hands deep in her pockets.)

MOM: I saw you! I saw you with Emily! I told you not to see her any more! Has this been going on for the past five months?

TEEN: God, Mom, what is your problem? We were just hang-ing out. *(Starts to walk away.)*

MOM: Don't walk away from me! Come here! Wait, what are you hiding? Give it to me! Give me your jacket.

TEEN: No! Wait, Mom, no!

MOM: No? I said give it to me, now.

TEEN: I don't have to give you anything —
(Mom is reaching for the jacket.)

TEEN: No! It's . . . it's *(Teen digs her nails into Mom's arm.)* Mine! *(Mom digs her nails into the back of Rachel's neck. She drops the jacket. Mom picks up the jacket and pulls out a small plastic bag of drugs from the pocket.)*

MOM: *(Screaming.)* What is this?

TEEN: *(Sassy.)* None of your business!

MOM: How dare you bring drugs into this house!

TEEN: I don't just bring them in the house, I take them, too! That's right! When you're not home, I'm getting high.

MOM: *(Mom slaps her hard.)* That's it! Go, get out of here!

TEEN: Go where?

MOM: I don't care. Just get out of my house. Go! You have ten minutes to get out of my sight.

RACHEL: Well, you always said that I would never forget my senior year. You were right. That was the year I got a job, the year I moved into a one-room apartment with people I didn't even know. Wow, looking back, I was really stupid. I gave up all I had for a life I didn't want. Days turned into weeks, weeks turned into months. At first, you would call almost ten times a day. Then, once a day, then once a week, then hardly at all.
(Teen is sitting down with her cell phone to her ear and we hear Mom's voice.)

MOM: All I want is for you to please come home. Please call back. *(Beep.)* Please come back home. Look, sweetie, I want to help you. Call me back. Bye. *(Beep.)* Hello, it's Mom again. Please call. Bye. *(Beep.)* Rachel, it's been almost two months. Please come home. *(Beep.)* It's Mom. You're welcome home, so please come back. *(Beep.)* Rachel, I want to work through this . . . I love you. *(Beep.)*

RACHEL: Finally, after four months, I had to go see you. Graduation came and went and the real world was here. I hadn't seen you at all, so just six weeks ago I stopped by the house.

MOM: *(She is sitting. There's a knock at the door. She shoots up and answers. She is talking to a friend of hers as if the friend is just off stage.)* Oh . . . I thought, I mean, it's you. No, no, I thought you were Rachel. You know what; I don't feel like going out tonight. Yes, yes, I know I haven't gone out in months, but I just feel like she's coming home, and I don't want to miss her. I know . . . I promise I'll go out next week. I just want to be alone, OK? Bye. *(Long pause. There is another knock on the door. She shoots up and then says to herself.)* Oh, why bother? I know it's not going to be *(She opens the door; Rachel walks onstage.)* Rachel!

TEEN: Hi . . . um I know I'm not supposed to be here but . . .

MOM: No, you can come in, sit down if you want.

TEEN: OK . . . *(Long pause.)* I was just in the neighborhood and thought maybe I should stop by.

MOM: That's good. I mean, it's nice to see you . . . Are you still in school and all that?

TEEN: Yep. I'm still in school, and I have a job now. I moved into the apartment building off of Painter Avenue, and I share an apartment with five others around my age.

MOM: Oh, that's nice. Um . . . are you sure that you have enough food? Do you need any money? Are you warm enough at night?

TEEN: Yes, yes, I'm doing fine, Mom.

MOM: Well, you know, sweetie, you are welcome home.

TEEN: Wait. I really came to say that . . . I'm moving out of state with Billy . . . a guy that lives in the same apartment building as me . . .

MOM: What? No sweetie, please move back with m . . .

TEEN: No, no, wait, Billy is a really nice guy, and he's moving back home to Ohio, and I'm going with him. He and I applied to Ohio State, and we start classes in two weeks.

MOM: But Rachel, I want you to move back here with me where you belong! You had the grades to get into UCS. If you stay out here, you can reapply in the fall.

TEEN: You're right. I HAD the grades. I kind of just slid by the last semester of school.

MOM: But Rachel, I thought you wanted more for yourself.

TEEN: Well, you thought wrong. I know I screwed up, but I want to fix it. I don't need you. I haven't needed you for the past four months.

MOM: *(Starting to tear up.)* Rachel, sweetheart, please move back home.

TEEN: No, this isn't my home anymore. I just stopped by to tell you I'm moving next week. Well, anyway, Billy's waiting in the car. Good-bye.

MOM: Wait, Rachel . . . I love you.

TEEN: Sure. OK, bye. *(Teen leaves. Mom quietly cries.)*

RACHEL: God, I wish I had talked to you more that day. I also wish I was nicer that day, but you can't take back the past; otherwise, we relive and regret. But, all in all, we had our ups and downs, and well, I wrote this to you to apologize for all the downs. I'm sorry for everything. I just wish I had written this earlier, or even better, told you in person. Now, it's a little late. I love you, Mom, with all my heart. Hope to see you . . . someday. Love, Rachel. *(She folds up the letter and turns it around to address it.)* Lot 43, Lawn of Rest, Rose Hills Cemetery, Whittier, California.

END OF PLAY

THE DREAM

2M, 2F

By Leah Prezioso
Bruton High School
Williamsburg, Virginia

Characters

JACK: Thirteen-year-old boy.
MOTHER: Jack's mother.
FATHER: Jack's father.
LYDIA: Jack's younger sister.

Setting

The entire play takes place in Jack's bedroom.

THE DREAM

Jack's bedroom. A twin-sized bed is placed center stage; adjacent to it, on the right, is a small, wooden nightstand with an alarm clock and a small, blue toy airplane. A wooden rocking chair is up stage right, visible to the audience. Jack charges angrily through the door, down stage left, and heads for his bed.

JACK: *(Yelling irritably while stomping through the door into his bedroom.)* Fine! I don't need you guys anyway! *(Once he reaches his bed, he sits in the center of it, cross-legged, facing the audience. He begins talking to himself, still angry.)* Grounded . . . Humph! Three times in one week! I should just run away or something . . . I bet they probably would not even notice! They would be so much happier without me; I just know it. No, I think that I should wait until morning. It's getting really late . . . and dark. *(He then yawns loudly and stretches his arms above his head.)* It doesn't help any that I'm so tired. You know, the rest of my family is most likely downstairs right now; just thinking about how much better life would be if I were not here. Sometimes, I just have to wonder . . . *(As his voice fades out, he yawns once more, lies down, and rolls onto his right side, facing the audience. He drifts off to sleep and into a dream. Approximately a minute later, Jack awakens to a blinding light coming from the doorway at down stage left. He sits up in his bed and peers toward the doorway with a quizzical look on his face. Mother, Father, and Lydia come through the door at down stage left and walk across the stage toward down stage right.)*

MOTHER: *(Trying to hold back tears.)* It has been exactly two years since Jack ran away from us. What if he's hurt, or hungry, or even killed? I wish he would just come back home. *(As she looks over to her husband, she begins to cry.)*

FATHER: *(Holding back a grim expression.)* Cheer up now darling. We are coming to the holiday seasons again, and just like in the past, we will get through it. *(Moving toward his wife, he puts his arm around her shoulders.)* And besides, we still have Lydia. *(Turns to look at his daughter.)* And that is something that we need to be thankful for.

LYDIA: Mother? Father? It is all my fault! *(She steps toward her parents, whimpering.)* I was so mean to Jack that night before he left! I'm the reason he left; he thinks that I hate him!

JACK: *(His voice shows desperation.)* Mom! Dad! Lydia! I'm right here. I never left you all; I am right here! *(Speaking to the audience now.)* Why can't they hear me? Why don't they answer me? I never left them. What are they talking about?

MOTHER: *(In a scolding, upset voice.)* Lydia, darling! Don't talk like that! *(Sighs.)* It was my fault. I'm the one who kept on arguing with him and told your father to ground him. I shouldn't have punished him so frequently. He was grounded three times in one week. *(Voice rising.)* In one week! If I had just sat him down and talked to him instead of punishing him so impatiently, he might still be here with us today, getting ready to celebrate the holidays as a family. This entire ordeal is completely my fault! *(Begins to cry again.)*

JACK: *(Sitting up even straighter now in bed, slightly frightened.)* No, Mother! It's not your fault at all. I am the one who kept on getting into trouble! Answer me Mother. Answer me! *(Speaking again to the audience.)* They can't hear me. I'm so confused! I just can't figure out if this is all a bad dream or if it's really happening to me.

FATHER: *(Sternly.)* Quiet down you two! Jack's running away is none of our faults. He decided it on his own. He will come back when he is ready to. My guess is that he thought that we didn't love him anymore. I can see why. None of us ever listened to him, and we weren't exactly very nice to him either. We also began to ground him for the smallest things that he did, so he most likely thought that he was no longer wanted in our family. *(Voice gets softer.)* I . . . I just wish that we could undo this whole thing and start completely over.

JACK: Oh, Father! You don't have to undo everything. I'm still here, and I never did run away. I don't understand what is going on. I can see and hear you, but you can't see or hear me. *(Looking toward the audience.)* None of this would have happened if I had just been the good son that my parents have always wanted me to be. I don't understand what is going on! I want everything to go back to normal! *(Turns from the audience and looks yearningly at his family.)*

LYDIA: Oh, Mother! If I had known that Jack was running away, I would have automatically turned into the best little sister he could ever ask for.

MOTHER: *(Sarcastically.)* Oh honey, don't worry about that. You are Jack's little sister. It's your job to annoy him. *(Sighs.)* I just wish he were back. I feel so guilty about all of this. I should have at least tried to be a more understanding parent . . . but now it's too late. The only person who can do something about all of this is Jack himself, and when he decides to come back to us, he will. I . . . I just know it . . . *(Pause.)* He has to . . . He's a part of this family and nothing can ever change that. We love him the way he is, but he has to realize that for himself now.

FATHER: *(Squeezing his wife's shoulder.)* He will, darling, and when that time finally comes, hopefully sooner than later, we will all welcome him with open hearts and arms. *(Smiles reassuringly at his daughter and ruffles her hair.)*

LYDIA: *(Whining.)* But Daddy! What if he doesn't come home? What if he decides that he doesn't love us anymore? He might not care about us any longer. And do you know what would be worst of all? If he has forgotten all about us and now he has a new family or something. Wouldn't that just be terrible? He hates us! I'm sure of it. If he hasn't come home by now, I don't think that he will ever be coming home! *(Turns away from her parents and starts to cry.)*

JACK: *(Talking to the audience.)* This is horrible! If this is a dream, would my family truly miss me this much if I did end up running away? Do I really mean this much to them? *(With speculation.)* I don't know . . .

FATHER: Come on Lydia, we need to find you something to do to get this all off your mind for a while. How about you help your mother fix dinner tonight? It's meatloaf night . . . mmm mmm!

MOTHER: *No*, we can eat leftovers later. All of this thinking about Jack has me worn out. I can't even begin to think of cooking dinner right now. Besides, it's only four, and we can wait another couple of hours.

FATHER: *(Looking at Mother in disbelief.)* Oh, right, uh . . . yeah . . . I guess dinner can wait. Honey, are you sure that you wouldn't like me to take you to the doctor? You seem to be extremely stressed out during this time of year.

MOTHER: *(Raising her voice.)* And you wonder why? How can you be so dense? Our son has run away! Does any of that ring a bell to you? I'm stressed because it's the winter holiday season, and we have to spend it without Jack. These holidays used to be such a special time for our family . . . I . . . I just can't bear to spend them without our son. Our small, once-loving family, now has an enormous gap in it that can only be filled with Jack, and unless he decides to come back, our family will never, ever be completely whole again.

JACK: *(Unable to restrain himself any longer, he attempts to jump out of his bed, only finding to his dismay, that he can't.)* Maybe this is all a dream if I can't even get out of bed, but it is so real! *(Turning to the audience.)* I shouldn't have even thought about running away in the first place, and then none of this would be happening. *(Sighing.)* I feel so stupid right now . . .

LYDIA: *(Excited.)* I know! I know! How about instead of talking about all of the bad things that have happened since Jack's running away, how about we tell stories of all the good times we had with him while he was here?

MOTHER: *(Overjoyed.)* Oh, Lydia! That's just a wonderful idea! It will definitely lighten up our dampened spirits. All right, who wants to go first? *(Looks back and forth between her husband and Lydia.)*

JACK: *(Rubbing his hands together in a sly way.)* Oh, yeah! This should be good.

LYDIA: *(Pleading.)* Mother! I want to go first! *(Jumping up and down excited.)* Pick me! Pick me!

MOTHER: *(Chuckling.)* All right, honey, you may go first.

LYDIA: *(She clears her throat.)* Well, I would like to tell of my best memory that I have ever shared with Jack. It was a sunny Friday afternoon, and Jack promised me that if I helped him do his weekly chores, he would teach me to ride a bicycle all by myself without training wheels. Between the both of us, we got his chores done in less than half an hour, and he took me out to the garage to disassemble my training wheels from my bike. We walked our bicycles to the top of the driveway and onto the sidewalk. Jack got on his bike and I got on mine. *(Pauses.)* He told me that if I followed his movements and paid attention to exactly what he was doing, that I'd learn how to ride my bike on the first try. I didn't even fall once! Jack was so proud of me, and we rode up and down Elm Street five times before we were both too exhausted to go on any further. Then he took me inside and put a Burger King crown on my head and called me the bicycle queen. That was probably the best day of my life that I can remember! *(Quietly.)* I wish Jack were here now so that we could go out and ride bikes together again.

MOTHER: Hush now darling. I really don't think that this whole storytelling business will keep us from thinking about how much we miss Jack. Maybe we should just go eat dinner now instead of waiting until later. All that I need to do is reheat some things and then it will be ready to be put on the table.

FATHER: *(Looks at his wife.)* Yeah, I think I agree with you on that one, honey. I'm starving!

LYDIA: *(Squeezes between her parents and grabs their hands.)* Mom, Dad? I think that even if Jack never comes back, I will love him forever and ever as a brother and as a friend.

MOTHER: *(Dabbing at tears.)* Oh, honey! That is about the nicest thing anyone could ever say to someone. If only Jack could hear you right now . . . *(The three of them walk hand in hand through the door at down stage left and disappear behind the curtain.)*

JACK: *(Grinning to himself.)* Lydia, I did hear you—loud and clear. And Mom was right: that was probably the nicest thing that anyone could have ever said to me. *(Looking toward the audience.)* I really think that was all just a dream, but it has definitely changed my mind about deciding to run away. I guess I never really thought about how much it would hurt my family to have me gone and completely out of their lives forever. I'm happy that this was all a dream instead of reality because I would have never thought of how much my family would actually miss me. Now that I've heard them say that they love me, I'm ashamed that I ever thought of leaving them, or of ruining their lives. Maybe tomorrow I'll reassure my family that I will never, ever leave them, and I will also tell them how much I love them. *(Yawns.)* I had better be getting to sleep because tomorrow is going to be a long, long day. *(Jack lies down and turns onto his right side, yawns and stretches one last time before he jumps up again, startled, at a loud knock coming from the door at down stage left. Door slowly opens, and Father peeks in first.)*

FATHER: Can we come in?

JACK: Yeah, I need to talk to all three of you anyway, preferably all at once. *(Father, Mother, and Lydia walk in one after the other and head toward center stage where Jack is sit-*

ting up in his bed. Father and Lydia are standing on the u stage center side of the bed, while Mother is standing, shifted to face the audience, at the center stage left side of the bed.)

FATHER: I have been talking to your mother, and we have decided that we all need to talk about everything that has been going on lately in this family. Now, we should start by tal . . . *(Jack cuts him off.)*

JACK: Dad, I really need to say something first. *(Clears his throat.)* I know that I haven't exactly been the perfect son that you have tried to raise me to be. But I just hate how I get into trouble all the time. It makes me so angry, and I even used to think about running away, until recently when I had this dream, if you want to call it that. And in it, you guys were so upset that I had run away, and you kept saying how much you missed me, and I just could not stand it. I have decided that it is not worth it to run away.

MOTHER: Oh, honey, we love you so much, and if you ever ran away, well, I just don't know how we would get through it. *(Reaches over and touches Jack's arm.)*

LYDIA: Exactly! And if you were gone, I wouldn't have an older brother to annoy, and you wouldn't be able to pick on me anymore. *(The family lightly laughs.)*

JACK: I know that now, and I also realized how much I am really loved by all of you, and if I were gone, our family would not be whole anymore. *(Grins and reaches over to ruffle Lydia's hair.)* Besides, I love all of you too, even if I have never told you so, and I still have no clue how the idea of running away ever crossed my mind. I do not think that I could ever imagine life without each of you by my side.

MOTHER: Well Jack, *(Looking at Father.)* you are our only son, and I do not think that we could ever imagine life without you here either. You mean so much to us, and I just cannot bear the thought of ever losing you. About this grounding business; I think that we were just trying to find an easy way out so that we would not have to sit down and talk about what you have done wrong every time something happens.

Maybe we could lay off on the grounding for a while; it has become way too overwhelming on your part if you have already begun thinking about running away.

JACK: Yeah, well, I am not going to argue with that! *(Looking sheepishly at his parents.)* I guess I would appreciate not being grounded so much. How about you yell at Lydia every once in a while?

LYDIA: *(Hands on her hips.)* Hey! That is so not fair! I am the good child, remember? I do not get into trouble.

FATHER: *(Laughing.)* Now, now, you two, stop quarreling. Jack? What are you doing in bed so early? We haven't even eaten dinner yet. Everybody, come on. Let's go eat that nice, warm meatloaf that I have been waiting for all day. Mmm Mmm!

MOTHER: *(Glancing toward the door at down stage left.)* Oh my, I forgot about that. The meatloaf is still in the oven; I hope it hasn't burned . . .

FATHER: All the more reason for us to hurry downstairs to eat it! Come on!

JACK: *(Thinking that there was no better time than the present.)* Mom? Dad? Lydia? I love you guys, and I always will, so never forget that, OK?

MOTHER: *(Lovingly.)* Jack, we love you, too, so you don't forget that either. *(A moment of silence.)* All right, let's go eat dinner — as a family.

(Jack climbs out of bed and grabs Lydia's hand, as well as Mother's. Father puts his arm across his wife's shoulders, and together, hand in hand, they walk happily down stage left from center stage to the door. Father opens it, and they all four walk out single file: Father, Mother, Jack, then Lydia. Once the door is shut again, the bedroom is quiet.)

END OF PLAY

THE DATE

2M, 2F

By Michael Kirsch
Orange County High School of the Arts
Santa Ana, California

Characters

NICK: A metrosexual teen who is a jock and knows a lot about fashion.

STEPHANIE: The dumb wannabe blond.

JUSTINE: A tomboy who tries really hard to be a girl.

SCOTT: A friend of Justine's who is a geeky teen.

Setting

The two scenes of two separate couples are played simultaneously. At play's end, the two couples run into each other and perform in one scene.

THE DATE

Two couples, Scott and Justine, stage right, and Nick and Stephanie, stage left.

STEPHANIE: Oh, my God! You like totally asked Justine the Saltine to the prom. Wait what?

NICK: Yeah, I kinda asked her out of pity. You should have seen her when I asked her. It was so funny.

STEPHANIE: She is pretty like me. Pretty desperate. *(Really annoying repetitive laugh.)*

NICK: Wow, you are frigging hilarious Stephanie. You should seriously get on the Comedy Sports Team.

STEPHANIE: Really, I should try out, yeah, and then I can finally get buff.

NICK: Stephanie, you are like so blond sometimes. Comedy Sports is a group where they . . . *(Stephanie gets distracted and walks off stage. Nick waits onstage, and Stephanie walks back on with a totally different outfit.)*

STEPHANIE: Hey . . .

NICK: That looks so much better.

STEPHANIE: I know!

NICK: You're welcome.

STEPHANIE: Please?

NICK: God, you are so hot right now. I really want to go to the prom with you and not the nasty Justine.

STEPHANIE: Yeah, you should go with me because I don't wear cheap stuff from Target. I do all my shopping at Kohl's.

NICK: Oh, my God! I am so going to try to go with you because I seriously can't be seen with her 'cause then I will have like no friends. I can just imagine what life would be about without friends.

(Nick stares off into the distance. Stephanie sits and puts

on makeup. The next scene between Justine and Scott starts while Nick and Stephanie freeze in place.)

SCOTT: We can talk about this forever Justine, but you will never ever convince me that you just got asked to the prom by Nick Kindley.

JUSTINE: I promise you, Scott, he just came up to me and said these exact words, "Will you go to the prom with me?"

SCOTT: How do you know he didn't say something like, . . . I don't know . . . something different than what he said?

JUSTINE: Don't be ridiculous, just because you haven't asked anyone yet doesn't mean that you have to be jealous.

SCOTT: I am not jealous. I just wish that you would stop lying to me.

JUSTINE: About what?

SCOTT: About Nick asking you. He is like the most popular guy in school and you're really hot . . . I mean not.

JUSTINE: What did you just say?

SCOTT: That you're not popular.

JUSTINE: No, before that.

SCOTT: That Nick is like the most popular guy in school.

JUSTINE: Don't be stupid Scott. You just called me hot.

SCOTT: No, no, I didn't.

JUSTINE: You did too Scott. You think I am hot!

SCOTT: I got to get to class, Justine.

JUSTINE: Jesus, Scott, it's the beginning of lunch. Just tell me the truth. Do you think I'm hot?

SCOTT: Well, you are kind of cute.

JUSTINE: That means that you find me attractive. Maybe so attractive that the whole reason why you were questioning me going with Nick is because the whole time you wanted to go to the prom with me.

SCOTT: Well . . .

JUSTINE: And you wanted to go with me and not one of your geeky friends.

SCOTT: I guess . . .

JUSTINE: And I need to not go to the prom with Nick because I find you extremely attractive also.

SCOTT: Well . . . Wait! What did you say?

JUSTINE: That you are extremely attractive and that I need to drop Nick as a date for the prom.

SCOTT: Yeah, that! Do you mean it? Like, seriously, you're not lying? Swear on God's life. You know if you're lying, you will go to hell.

JUSTINE: Yeah.

SCOTT: Oh, my gosh!

JUSTINE: Yeah!

SCOTT: Oh, my gosh!

JUSTINE: Yeah!

SCOTT: Oh, my gosh!

(Switch back to Nick and Stephanie's scene in which they now have to come up with a plan to not go to the prom with Justine.)

NICK: Oh, my God! I was totally like daydreaming. OK, you seriously have to go and get me out of going to the prom with Justine. I really want to go with you.

STEPHANIE: Why do you want to go with me Nick? Is it because you don't like Justine?

NICK: Stephanie, we already went over this. She is nasty, and she also smells like burnt cheese.

STEPHANIE: Yeah.

NICK: So?

STEPHANIE: So what?

NICK: What should I do to get out of going to the prom with Justine?

STEPHANIE: Oh, my God! Best idea ever. Why don't you distract her while I see what size shirt she wears. Then I could like go and see what size pants she wears. I could also find the type of brand. We could use that information to our advantage and then . . .

NICK: OK, Stephanie, you're freaking me out. You sounded

smart. OK, I think I have an idea. Why don't I pretend that I'm gay so then she'll think I like guys.

STEPHANIE: Nick, that is so gross. You like guys?

NICK: No! I am pretending to be gay. Also, Stephanie, you like guys?

STEPHANIE: Oh, yeah!

NICK: I think I'm just going to walk up and tell her.

STEPHANIE: Tell her what?

NICK: Listen, I will tell you one more time. I am going to pretend that I am gay so that Justine thinks that I like guys and not chicks. So that way she will feel awkward to go to a dance as a date with a gay guy.

STEPHANIE: That would so work so well.

NICK: OK, I'm going to go and tell her right now.

(Starts to walk then freezes to start Justine and Scott's scene, where they now have to find a way for Justine to not go to the prom with Nick.)

JUSTINE: Stay calm. *(Both gather themselves.)*

SCOTT: Justine, oh I am so happy you feel the same way.

JUSTINE: Whoa, one problem before we go on from here. How are we going to drop Nick?

SCOTT: Oh, yeah. I totally forgot about that situation.

JUSTINE: OK, I have an idea and it involves you.

SCOTT: Justine, anything for you my PD.

JUSTINE: What does that mean, Scott?

SCOTT: My PD. My prom date.

JUSTINE: OK, if you are going to be my date, don't ever talk like that ever again or I will seriously drop kick you so hard.

SCOTT: OK. Sorry sweetheart, babykins, honey bear.

JUSTINE: Stop it.

SCOTT: Jeez, sorry.

JUSTINE: We need to think of this situation seriously, Scott. So back to the situation that involves you. I think you should fight Nick.

SCOTT: Whoa, Whoa. I won't do that for you.

JUSTINE: OK, fine then. So much for, "Oh I'd do anything for you, my PD."

SCOTT: I have an idea. We could just come up with a story.

JUSTINE: Yeah, and it could have something to do with me getting sick.

SCOTT: No, too easy.

JUSTINE: Oh, how about my car got in a crash so we can't drive to the prom.

SCOTT: Oh, my God, you have a gift for coming up with ideas. *(Sarcastically.)* You are taking a limo to the prom.

JUSTINE: Oh, my gosh. I totally forgot. Maybe I should go with Nick?

SCOTT: *(Whining.)* Justine?

JUSTINE: Just kidding.

SCOTT: No more coming up with the story. I have got the best idea ever. We get him sick. Yeah, and then he can't go to the prom because he got so sick he has to stay home. But what sickness can get you sick enough to stay home from your own prom?

JUSTINE: Food poisoning?

SCOTT: Yeah!

JUSTINE: We could poison his food at lunch. When he's staring at my luscious face, you can drop rat poisoning in his sandwich.

SCOTT: Won't that kill him?

JUSTINE: Probably, ummm . . . .Wait! I know. My dad bought Ipecac after my mom had food poisoning from that one seafood restaurant, and we could use that to make him throw up.

SCOTT: But it will only make him throw up.

JUSTINE: Yeah, but he will be throwing up so much that he will think he is sick. *(Pause.)* No wait! Better idea. What if it is as simple as I tell him that I'm a lesbian?
(Nick and Stephanie have approached Scott and Justine and are standing right behind them.)

SCOTT: Ummm . . . Justine?

JUSTINE: He is standing right behind me, isn't he? *(Scott nods his head.).*

JUSTINE: Hey!

NICK: Hey!

NICK and JUSTINE: *(Simultaneously.)* I have something to tell you.

JUSTINE: I'm into girls!

NICK: I'm into guys!

STEPHANIE and SCOTT: Ewww!

NICK: So . . . about the prom?

JUSTINE: Guess we shouldn't go together now, huh?

NICK: Guess not.

SCOTT: Hey, Stephanie . . . do you have a date? Want to go with me?

JUSTINE: Scott!

STEPHANIE: Please, get over yourself. I'm going with Nick.

JUSTINE: But I thought you were gay?

NICK: I'm sorry, Justine. I'm not really gay. I'd just rather go with Stephanie. She's hot.

JUSTINE: Fine. I'd rather go with Scott.

SCOTT: Really?

NICK: Really?

STEPHANIE: I think they make a cute couple.

NICK: So, it's all good, right?

JUSTINE: I guess, yeah.

SCOTT: Hey, you guys . . . wanna all go together in the same limo?

(Pause.)

JUSTINE, STEPHANIE, NICK: No!

END OF PLAY

SIMPLY LOVE

3M, 4F

By Kelynda Hepburn
Santa Barbara, California

Characters

CHANELLE MONTGOMERY: Sixteen. Self-confident. Narrator of the story and the ultimate best friend. Should have a very "character role" look to contrast with Melissa.

MELISSA GAVINS: Sixteen. A fresh, pretty ingénue; very romantic but happy to wait for her Prince Charming. Though naïve and innocent, she is feisty and fun.

JASON MILES: Seventeen. Kindhearted and caring, but very anxious to be liked by his peers. When he's alone with Melissa, he is at ease and comfortable. Around other students, he is careful with himself and wears a mask of "carefree, normal teenagerness" to protect himself.

CASSIE SCARETT: Eighteen. Tall, thin, and self-confident. She has a studied sensuality, imitated from hundreds of chick flicks and teen dramas. Not mean or intentionally cruel, but mostly out for herself in life.

MS. ELEGANTIA MICHELANGELO: French acting teacher. Late fifties to mid-sixties; tall, slender. Talented, but a bit scatterbrained.

PHILIP ACKERMAN: Seventeen. Flamboyant and possibly homosexual. Charming, witty, sweet, attractive; a romantic-lead look.

AARON FREDERICHS: Eighteen. Blond and buff; a ladies' man.

Note: Chanelle, Melissa, Jason, Cassie, and Philip also play their adult selves (mid- to late twenties).

SIMPLY LOVE

Lights come up on Chanelle, a high school girl standing in a down stage corner. This is Chanelle's "corner," for future reference.

CHANELLE: This is a story about people. They were in high school together, in the drama department. They were theater people. Theater, where the line between reality and pretend is often blurred and sometimes abruptly snapped in two. Wow . . . that was really deep. I'm Chanelle, by the way, in case you were wondering, which you probably weren't. Melissa and Jason were friends, best friends. Let me clarify that word for you again . . . best *friends*. They were just like each other . . . the same person in two different bodies. Screw that whole thing about opposites attracting. They were like each other, and so they understood each other. He could tell when she was stressed out; she knew when he was upset. And . . . well, I'll just let you watch . . .
(Lights come up on Melissa and Jason, sitting on the floor, sharing an iPod. Neither of them moves. They simply sit staring off into nowhere, clearly focusing on the music. The song ends, and they pull the earphones off their ears.)

MELISSA: Good song.

JASON: Yeah, I thought so. I really like the harmonies at the end.

MELISSA: Yeah, me too. And those weird little rifts he does at the beginning. That gave me chills.

JASON: *(Glancing at his watch.)* Oh, shoot, we better get to class.
(A group of students, including Chanelle, amass on the other side of the stage, forming a classroom. Melissa and Jason enter the classroom, where a group of "theater geeks" are sitting in chairs waiting for their instructor to arrive. As Melissa and Jason enter, a tall, slender girl stands up and

runs over, throwing her arms around Jason, while greeting both of them.)

CASSIE: Hi guys!

MELISSA: *(A little awkwardly, but still friendly.)* Hey, Cassie! She here yet?

CASSIE: *(Glancing at her.)* Still in the office. *(Grabbing his arm, clearly excluding Melissa without meaning to.)* So, Jason, I wanted to talk to you about . . . *(They cross back to the other students, where we see she has saved a seat for him.)*.

MELISSA: *(Crossing over to Chanelle, who is reading a book, giving her a hug, and sitting down.)* Hey, Nel.

CHANELLE: *(Looking up from her book and smiling.)* Hey, Mel. Well . . . I asked him.

MELISSA: You . . . you did not!

CHANELLE: Yep.

MELISSA: You asked a boy to the prom? That . . . that just isn't right!

CHANELLE: No, it's not. But I did it. And BTW, I didn't ask just any boy! I asked Aaron Frederichs! *(They both look over at an attractive blond boy sitting among a group of girls, one of whom is massaging his shoulders.)*

MELISSA: My gosh! Well . . .

CHANELLE: Well, what?

MELISSA: *(Like a little kid on Christmas.)* Well, what did he say?

CHANELLE: He said he doesn't know. He already "kind of promised" at least half a dozen other girls, so he has to make sure they all have dates before he says yes to me.

MELISSA: But he wants to go with you?

CHANELLE: Yeah, he does. We're like *made* for each other! We've got this . . . chemistry isn't the right word. *(Melissa laughs.)* It's like . . . magic. You know, like you and Jason.

MELISSA: *(Suddenly becoming very serious.)* Me and Jason? Heck no, girl! We're just . . . similar . . . that's all. He's like my brother, ya know?

CHANELLE: *(Sighing.)* Yeah, sure. That's why you'll say no if he asks you to the prom, right?

MELISSA: *(Taken aback.)* He's gonna ask me to the prom?

CHANELLE: I hear things . . .

(The entire class stands and begins to cheer as an attractive older woman, Ms. Elegantia Michelangelo, enters the room. She proceeds to bow and curtsy in a theatrical manner. She is tall and skinny, and her long, dark hair is pulled up in a French twist. She is very refined, but not very organized, and she loves to entertain. She wears form-fitting, artsy clothing and big dangling earrings. The entire class stays standing until she sits down, and then they sit.)

MS. MICHELANGELO: *(In a very grand sort of way.)* Hello, young ladies and gentlemen. All right, start your relaxation, while I talk to you about next week.

(The entire class lies down on the floor, eyes closed, breathing deeply.)

MS. MICHELANGELO: As you know, we are putting on a spring musical a month from now. To save time, we are using your drama class time next week to facilitate auditions. *(She pulls a typed piece of paper out of her briefcase and begins to read.)* Musical auditions will be with Joe on Tuesday. Please bring a contrasting ballad and up-tempo, sixteen bars of each. Bring sheet music or a background tape. On Wednesday, you will be reading sides with me! Also, bring a contemporary monologue, just in case. *(She sets the paper down.)*. All right then, young ladies and gentlemen, you're prepared, you know what to do! So, let's get started on our exercises, shall we?

(The class continues to progress silently, as Chanelle steps forward to her corner again.)

CHANELLE: I'm sure you're all wondering what musical we put on. Well, I'm not going to tell you. It really doesn't matter. What matters is that you know that Melissa and Philip . . . Oh, shoot, you don't know who Philip is, do you? Doesn't matter, you'll meet him in just a sec . . . Well, anyway, they were perfect for the romantic leads in the show, while Cassie and Jason were just right for the secondary leads. Ironic, isn't it?

(The class is over. Melissa and Chanelle gather up their back-packs and books. Philip runs up to them, picking Melissa up and spinning her around in a heart-melting way.)

PHILIP: *(Very excited.)* Hey, sweetie. Do you think they'll allow duets on Tuesday? We could do that one . . .

MELISSA: Yeah, that would be fun! I'm sure they'd allow it. The leads only sing duets anyway.

PHILIP: Great! OK, you wanna work the arrangement with Joe after class tomorrow?

MELISSA: Sure. Sounds vahnderful, dahling.

PHILIP: Mahvelous! *(He bounds away.)*.

(Melissa and Chanelle stare after him admiringly for a long, awkward pause. Then, Chanelle sneezes, and it breaks their trance.)

CHANELLE: Sweet guy.

MELISSA: Yeah, too bad he's gay.

(They exit the classroom, arms linked, and proceed to where the lockers are.)

CHANELLE: *(Giving her a hug good-bye.)* All right, see ya to-morrow, Mel!

MELISSA: OK, Nel, see ya tomorrow.

(She opens her locker and jams her books into her back-pack. Jason walks over, carrying an overpacked backpack, leaning forward from its weight.)

JASON: Hey.

MELISSA: *(Smiling.)* Hey.

JASON: *(Tired.)* You think your mom can give me a ride home?

MELISSA: Sure, you're on our way home. *(She finishes packing her backpack and closes her locker, slumping against the wall, staring into nowhere.)* But, um . . . she's gonna be a little late. Is that OK?

JASON: Mmm-hmm. No hurry. *(He slumps next to her, not look-ing at her either, but not in an awkward way. This is just how they talk to each other.)* So, you decided on an essay topic?

MELISSA: Yep.

JASON: You gonna tell me what it is or make me guess?

MELISSA: It's on my perfect mate. *(She makes a barely notice-able glance toward him.)*.

JASON: Interesting. *(Trying to be nonchalant.)* And what would he consist of?

MELISSA: *(Laughing.)* That's a funny way of putting it. Hmmm . . . well, I haven't thought about it much.

JASON: You're lying. You think about it a lot.

MELISSA: *(Defensively, but still lightly.)* And how would you know?

JASON: You're a romantic . . . *(He waits, not sure if he wants to add the next statement.)* like me.

MELISSA: *(Her eyes light up, but she tries to maintain an aura of aloofness.)* He has to be able to sing.

JASON: Sing?

MELISSA: *(Getting excited: we know she has thought about this a lot.)* Yes, and dance. And . . . *(Grabbing at the cross around her neck.)* he *has* be a Christian, obviously.

JASON: *(He gently fingers the cross around his neck.)* Mmm-hmm . . . *(Quietly, trying not to appear too interested.)* What else?

MELISSA: He has to treat me like a princess. *(Jason rolls his eyes.)* I know; it sounds so . . .

JASON: Cliché?

MELISSA: *(She agrees, but still wants to be a princess.)* I suppose . . . and . . . he has to be smart and charming and witty, and *(Building.)* he has to know how to cook, and *(With a toss of her head.)* he has to like books!

JASON: *(Thoroughly enjoying her enthusiasm.)* Hmmm . . . *(Still trying to hide his interest.)* That sounds like a lot for a man to be. A lot to live up to . . .

MELISSA: *(Sneakily.)* Why? Who wants to?

JASON: *(Trying not to, but it slips.)* . . . Do you want me to?

(Melissa is shocked and speechless at this sudden outburst. She is saved by the sound of a car horn.)

MELISSA: *(Standing up.)* That's my mom.

JASON: *(Grateful as well.)* Yeah.

(They exit. Blackout. Lights come up on the class. Melissa is chatting excitedly with Philip as Cassie giggles flirtatiously at Jason's not very funny jokes. Chanelle is in her corner again.)

CHANELLE: OK, so it's audition week. We had our music auditions on Tuesday. Pretty normal outcome. Philip and Melissa's duet was cute. Everybody said so. Jason found this amazing ballad and pulled it off without ever having run it with an accompanist before. Cassie sang an overdone uptempo, but managed to make it her own. And me? I was OK. Then it was time to run our sides. Everybody in the class had a pretty good idea already of who was playing who, and we all thought the second half of the audition was basically pointless. But of course, things didn't occur as expected. If they did, why the heck would I be telling this story?

(Sometime during this monologue, Ms. Michelangelo enters the room, and the class again does its stand-and-cheer routine. Ms. Michelangelo again bows and curtsies, then sits, and the class sits as well. They then begin to act out the next part of Chanelle's monologue.)

CHANELLE: Ms. Michelangelo first asked Melissa and *Jason* to go up and read a scene that takes place between the two romantic leads. They got up in front of everyone *without their script,* being the overachievers that they were. They proceeded to do the scene in a polite, well-acted manner. It was nice, but a bit standoffish, and nowhere near the stage chemistry that Melissa and Philip always created. Oh, and don't think Melissa and Jason were in any way awkward around each other since last week's conversation. They were both happy to pretend it had never happened. Everything was *fine,* until Melissa remembered a set of stage directions. *(Chanelle enters back into the scene.).*

MELISSA: Ummm . . . I'm supposed to faint here, and he's supposed to catch me. Did you want us to do that now?

MS. MICHELANGELO: *(Annoyed that Melissa has broken character.)* Of course!

MELISSA: Should I just . . .

MS. MICHELANGELO: Just do it!

(She does. It is perfectly natural and realistic. Jason catches her out of sheer reflex, but can't help feeling somewhat romantic as he lifts her up and carries her to the "bed." He stares at her, completely overwhelmed and in the moment. He is supposed to be saying a line. Several of the kids snicker, and it breaks the spell.)

JASON: Oh! Uh . . . line!

MS. MICHELANGELO: Rest . . .

JASON: Um . . . rest, my darling. *(Breaking character.)* Should I? *(Ms. Michelangelo gives him an agitated glance and wave of her hand. He sighs, somewhat reluctant to follow stage directions, sits on the bed, leans down, and kisses Melissa. She opens her eyes, surprised, but pulls herself up and kisses him back. The entire class lets out a couple of gasps, woohoo's, and catcalls. Melissa and Jason pull back from each other, both shocked. They then proceed to act like it was nothing, simply a stage direction.)*

MS. MICHELANGELO: Well! That was brilliant! Not exactly how I would have interpreted it, but nevertheless brilliant! *(Jason and Melissa go back to their chairs. Chanelle gives Melissa a little punch in the arm, and then returns to her corner. The class proceeds with more auditions, but silently acting out the story given by Chanelle.)*

CHANELLE: Yeah, it really happened. But here's where it gets juicy. Ms. Michelangelo then proceeded to run the same scene with several more couples. Me and Aaron. Then, Philip and Melissa. Now, Melissa was rather embarrassed by her actions in her previous scene with Jason. So, to prove that her "passionate kiss" had nothing to do with her feelings toward Jason, she kissed Philip in the exact same way. Well, Jason was rather hurt by the fact that Melissa could turn her romance on and off like a water faucet. But, being an actor, he was able to hide it. Ms. Michelangelo called the next couple, Jason and Cassie. Cassie was excited, to say the least. They went up onstage . . . and Jason succeeded in playing the perfect lover. When they got to the kissing part, he was prepared to show the classroom that his acting skills were just as good as Melissa's. As he leaned in to kiss Cassie . . . well, watch what happened . . .

(Jason sits on the bed next to a fainted Cassie. She sits up, throwing her arms around him and pulling him on top of her in a very sexy, yet very unromantic kiss. Still, as they pull apart, it is very clear that Jason, as well as Cassie, very much enjoyed it. If he wasn't already, he has clearly become attracted to her in that one moment. They go back to their chairs.)

CHANELLE: Well, um . . . I don't think that needs any explaining. Anyway, you don't want to see the rest of the auditions, do you? No, I didn't think so . . . you saw all of the important parts.

(Chanelle walks back into the scene. Seeing that Melissa looks a bit downcast, she gives her hand a squeeze. They gather up their backpacks and books. Arms around each other, they go to the lockers. Chanelle gives Melissa a hug and exits. Melissa watches Jason and Cassie enter, absorbed in conversation about the auditions. It is clear that Melissa wants to talk to Jason, but not with Cassie around. She slowly begins packing her backpack, waiting for the right moment to butt into the conversation. Philip runs up and grabs her around the waist.)

PHILIP: Well, I think that went well, don't you? We are *so* playing the leads! No one else even came close!

MELISSA: *(Very tired.)* Yeah.

PHILIP: What's wrong?

MELISSA: Oh, nothing. *(Seeing there is a break in Jason and Cassie's conversation.)* Just a sec. Jason!

JASON: Yeah?

MELISSA: You um . . . *(She glances at Cassie, then turns back to him, awkwardly and somewhat desperately.)* . . . you want a ride home?

JASON: *(Cold and quick, trying to hurt Melissa, but caring more about how he looks in front of Cassie.)* No, I'm good. Thanks.

MELISSA: Oh, OK.

(She backs away and watches as he gathers his stuff together. He turns to Cassie, thoroughly engrossed in entertaining her.)

JASON: Shall we?

(Cassie giggles and grabs his hand. They start to exit. Jason by this point has completely forgotten that Melissa is behind him.)

JASON: *(To Cassie.)* So, you . . . um . . . going with anyone to the prom yet?

(They exit. Melissa stands, frozen, not sure at all how to handle the situation. She slumps to the ground and begins to cry. Philip, who she has completely forgotten about, walks toward her, kneels down, and puts his hand on her shoulder in a comforting gesture. She turns, embarrassed that someone has caught her crying, but gives in, glad to have arms to fall into. Blackout.)

(Lights come up. The stage is empty. Chanelle walks in wearing a stunning evening gown, full-length gloves, hair pulled up. She carries a chair, sets it in her corner, and sits down legs crossed, one arm over the back. She is now an adult, but basically the same Chanelle that we know. It is ten years later.)

CHANELLE: The show was a hit. I'm sure you already know who was cast. Melissa and Philip were the leads. Cassie and Jason were the secondary leads. I was the narrator. After the prom, Jason and Cassie dated all through high school. Melissa never drove Jason home or shared an iPod with him again. They grew farther and farther apart. Now, it's ten years later. I got married. No, not to Aaron Frederichs. He's had about four wives by now. I married this guy, Harold Schmidt, that I met in freshman anatomy. We're both doctors. Melissa performed on Broadway at nineteen. She was a complete unknown. Starred in a musical and completed college at the same time. I, of course, attended both her opening and closing performances, and a couple in between. Now she's on tour performing cabarets across the country. Philip sings all of her duets with her. He ended up marrying their accompanist, Jillian Fairfield. Yeah . . . you heard right, she's a woman! Jason and Cassie stayed long-distance lovers while he got his BFA in musical theater at NYU and she became a model. And they . . . well, I'll just let you watch.

(During this monologue, a fancy New York nightclub has materialized behind her. Women in evening gowns and men in tuxedos are sitting at tables. Musicians are onstage, setting up microphones and instruments. Chanelle sits at a table. Philip, now an adult, is dressed in a tuxedo. He walks up to one of the microphones.)

PHILIP: Ladies and gentlemen. Thank you for coming tonight. We hope it'll be worth your while, and now, without further ado, the girl you've all been waiting for, Miss Melissa Gavins!

(Melissa sweeps in, stunning in a long dress. She steps up to the microphone opposite Philip. As she begins to sing, Jason and Cassie enter the room.)

MELISSA:*(To Philip.)* Every time you say you love me, every time you hold my hand, I melt a little inside. I feel that I'm losing my mind. And I'm going crazy. And I . . .

(She sees Cassie and Jason and stops, fixated on the couple. Jason is handsomely dressed in a tuxedo and gloves. Cassie, on his arm, wears an ornate tiara, and her low-cut gown features her obviously fake breasts. Melissa is filled with a cacophony of emotions: surprise, delight, and dis-

appointment each take a turn at shading her face. Jason is equally surprised at seeing her. Cassie is all smiles, having planned the entire surprise herself, obviously not at all threatened by Melissa's presence.)

PHILIP: *(Suddenly understanding Melissa's speechlessness, he runs over to the piano, covering for the sudden silence of his partner.)* Oops! Would you look at that; we're missing a page of sheet music! Why don't we take a short break . . . enjoy the champagne.

CASSIE: *(To the shocked Jason.)* Well, I told you we were going to see an old friend, didn't I?

JASON: Well . . . yes. But I didn't realize . . .

PHILIP: Why don't we all go back to the dressing room?
(They cross to a down stage corner, which has transformed into a dressing room, complete with a couch and dressing table. Melissa sits at the dressing table, busying herself with her makeup, trying desperately not to make eye contact with Jason. Philip stands next to her, as Cassie pulls Jason onto the couch with her.)

CASSIE: Isn't it wonderful? Now we're all together again, just like old times. *(Clearly for Melissa's sake.)* Well, not exactly like old times.

MELISSA: *(Nervously.)* And why not?

CASSIE: Well . . . why don't you tell them, dear?

JASON: *(Quietly, as if confessing a sin.)* We're . . . getting married.

MELISSA: *(Letting her composure slip.)* Married? *(Back to her actress self.)* Well, that's wonderful. Absolutely wonderful. Just . . . *(She is desperately holding back tears, maintaining a smile.).*

PHILIP: *(Nonchalantly playing the matchmaker.)* Well, I'll take Cassie out to see Chanelle and her husband. And you two can . . . catch up on memories.

CASSIE: Yes. You should. Jason and I are moving to California after the wedding. We got a movie deal together! Isn't that wonderful?

MELISSA: Wonderful . . . *(Suddenly realizing that she will be left alone in the room with Jason.)* Wait . . . *(She begs Philip with her eyes not to leave her.)*

PHILIP: *(Nodding his head at her in a "father knows best" manner and pushing Cassie out toward the tables.)* Just remember, you've got a number in fifteen minutes.

MELISSA: But . . .

(As he exits, she stands as if to follow him, but her knees buckle underneath her. Jason stands as if to catch her, but she defiantly steadies herself on the dressing-table chair. She is breathing shallowly and with difficulty. She eases herself back into her chair.)

JASON: *(Afraid to ask.)* You all right?

MELISSA: *(Snaps.)* Fine! It's . . . this stupid corset. *(Forgetting her anger for a moment.)* My manager says skinny minnies are in! He says the boys like it.

JASON: Oh, I've always preferred curves on a woman.

MELISSA: *(Indicating back toward the tables.)* Yeah, I noticed.

JASON: Oh, no. That was her idea. For the whole . . . Hollywood thing.

MELISSA: *(Letting it slip, with the knowledge that she will never see him again anyway.)* Does she love you?

JASON: *(Caught off guard.)* What? Well, yes . . . yes, of course she does.

MELISSA: No, I mean does she love *you*? The good and the bad?

JASON: *(Clearly having never thought about this before.)* Well . . .

MELISSA: Like, does she love the way you get neurotic before an audition? Or how you shut yourself in and listen to dark, scary musicals on your iPod really loudly when you're upset. Or how you pretend not to care what other people think of you, but really let them dictate a lot of who you are when you're with them? Or how you get really quiet when you haven't had enough sleep? Does she love any of that? Or does she just know you have good looks and that you're "fun to be with"? And, more importantly, is that all that's important to you? Is that all romance means to you? I thought I knew you better than that, Jason.

JASON: Look, if this is about the prom all those years ago . . .

MELISSA: Oh, Jason, don't be stupid. I knew why you didn't invite me to the prom. I wasn't a nice arm decoration to match your pretty face, that's all.

JASON: Wait, now, that's not fair . . .

MELISSA: Isn't it? That's all you're worth now, isn't it? Your pretty face. She's eaten up the rest of you. There's nothing left inside. Now, if you'll excuse me, I need to be onstage.

(She takes as deep a breath as she can get in the corset, turns on her inner actress, and walks toward the stage. Jason, defeated and angry, stands and brushes past her. He crosses to Cassie, pulling her away from Chanelle and Philip.)

JASON: Come on, babe. Let's go. I'm sick of this place.

PHILIP: *(Realizing what is happening, he pretends to have a "frog in his throat.")* Oh, but um . . . Jason. I can't do this next number with Mel. My voice is completely gone. Could you do it with her before you go? I'd so appreciate it. You know "Simply Love," don't you?

JASON: *(Brusquely.)* No, I couldn't . . . I really must be going.

PHILIP: Oh, please! I know Mel would love it.

JASON: Oh, I doubt that.

CASSIE: *(Still unthreatened.)* Come on, Jason. Be a sport.

JASON: No, I . . .

(Philip pulls him over toward the stage, as Melissa begins to sing. She is pale, and throughout the song, we see her grow weaker and weaker.)

MELISSA: A girl, a boy. A first dance. A kiss on the porch. And they were in love

(Philip pushes Jason onto the stage.)

JASON: Sweet smiles and flowers. *(Melissa bewilderedly avoids eye contact, afraid that she'll break and cry.)* Weeks filled with laughter. Dreams and ambitions, shared together.

(Philip goes to sit with Chanelle.)

CHANELLE: *(Suspiciously.)* So . . . what was wrong with your voice?

PHILIP: *(Smiling.)* Nothing. Absolutely nothing.

MELISSA and JASON: *(Both desperately trying not to look at each other, but wanting to.)* They wish and want; And hope and dream; Their days go by, in a blur.

(Jason grabs her hand, in a gesture of apology.)

MELISSA: *(Falling for him all over again.)* All she can do is think about him.

JASON: *(Smiling that she has forgiven him.)* And he the same with her.

(Melissa gasps. Her knees buckle under her, and she faints. Jason catches her. He slowly lifts her into his arms and carries her off stage. Cassie tries to get up and follow him in protest, but Philip holds her down, and Chanelle sits in her lap.)

CHANELLE: *(As the narrator again, holding Cassie down.)* I suppose I should be narrating this next part, but I'm a little busy here. That's all right; it's pretty self explanatory, don't you think?

(Jason carries Melissa into her dressing room and lays her down on the couch. He sits next to her, gazing at her face. Slowly and nervously he leans toward her, in the same way he did ten years ago. Impulsively, he kisses her quickly, then pulls away to search for a reaction of some sort. We see Melissa smile and open her eyes. She slowly sits up, her eyes fixed on his face. She throws her arms around his neck, and they kiss passionately.)

END OF PLAY

THE STALLS

1M, 3F

By Kendall Mauvezin
The California Conservatory of the Arts
San Juan Capistrano, California

Characters

CARA: An insecure teenage girl who hates her nose.
PENNY: A loud and confident teenage girl
JONATHAN: A sassy and loud teenage boy who is completely comfortable with himself.
MAGGIE: A popular girl who is covering up deep insecurities.

Setting

Cara is in a bathroom stall listening to Maggie and a few other girls who are making fun of Cara's nose. Soon after, Cara leaves the stall. Penny, and later Jonathan, enter the bathroom to plan their next move against Maggie.

THE STALLS

At rise, Cara exits the bathroom stall, hearing Maggie's final words as she exits the bathroom.

MAGGIE: How sad . . . I don't know what I'd do if I had such a huge nooo . . .
(Maggie is cut off by the slamming of the bathroom door).
CARA: *(Looking at herself in the mirror.)* OH, MY GOSH!
(Cara's best friend Penny loudly enters the bathroom.)
PENNY: Hey, Care Bear! I was looking for ya. Do you know what's for lunch today?
CARA: *(To herself.)* I knew I never liked my nose.
PENNY: Hey, Care, ummm . . . what does that have anything to do with what's for lunch today?
CARA: Maggie! That's what this has to do with lunch.
PENNY: *(Laughs.)* What? That makes no sense.
(Jonathan enters.)
JONATHAN: Why, hello friends. I thought I might find you in here. Cara, yellow is such a good color for you.
PENNY: *(Giving Jonathan a weird look.)* OK. So Cara, why don't you tell me one more . . .
(Penny is interrupted by Jonathan who coughs and shoots her a dirty look.)
PENNY: Fine. Tell *us* one more time what's going on.
JONATHAN: *(To Penny.)* Thank you.
PENNY: *(To Jonathan.)* Of course.
CARA: I heard her!
JONATHAN: Heard who, hon?
CARA: Maggie! Maggie and all her stupid little blond friends.
PENNY: What?
CARA: They were talking about my nose. I heard it! I was in the last stall listening to them laugh, and as I walked out I heard her. You can quote me on this. *(In a really high and annoying*

voice.) "How sad. I don't know what I'd do if I had such a huge nooo . . . "

PENNY: What?

JONATHAN: Oh, no! She did not!

PENNY: Yes. Yes, she did.

JONATHAN: I do not think this girl knows who she's dealing with.

PENNY: Well then, maybe we should inform her.

CARA: Thanks, guys. But Maggie's right. I do have a huge nose. Or should I say, huge beak? I have a big, fat bird nose, and you know it! From now on just call me . . .

JONATHAN: *(Interrupting.)* Oh please . . . don't do it . . .

CARA: Tucci.

PENNY: OK. Let's just leave him out of this, shall we?

CARA: Why? Come on guys, let's face it. Soon it'll just be me and him. Me and Tucci. Cara, the bird-nosed girl, and Tucci, the dog-faced boy. We make a great pair, don't you think?

JONATHAN: Hon, you know we'd never let that happen.

PENNY: Maggie Patterson is a fat cow! We won't let her get away with this.

(Maggie enters the bathroom immediately following Penny's comment.)

MAGGIE: Won't let who get away with what?

(They all turn to see Maggie.)

PENNY: Listen, Miss Maggie, if you think for one second that you can just . . .

JONATHAN: *(Interrupting as he inspects Maggie's outfit.)* Wait a minute. Where did you get your shirt?

MAGGIE: Oh, um . . . I . . . .um . . . I'm not sure. *(Readjusting herself.)* Why? Don't you just love it?

JONATHAN: No, as a matter of fact, I don't. That's why I stole it from my sister and threw it away. I wanted to burn it, but my mom wouldn't let me.

PENNY: How did Maggie get it then?

JONATHAN: Good question. Why don't you tell us . . . Miss Maggie?

MAGGIE: No.

PENNY: Oh, wow. Did you go through their trash? Did the princess actually go through someone's trash and is wearing a hand-me-down?

MAGGIE: No! There's no way. You people are crazy. *(She becomes increasingly uncomfortable.)* God . . . get a life and leave me out of it.

JONATHAN: *(Laughing.)* Oh . . . and see that snag on the shoulder? That's where I stopped my sister from cutting up the collar while she was going through that *(In a high, mocking voice.)* "I hate the world, and the world hates me," *(Changing back to his normal voice.)* or whatever you call it, stage.

CARA: Oh, my gosh! It is her shirt. It totally is. You're right, Jono.

PENNY: *(To Jonathan.)* Quite impressive detective work, sunshine.

JONATHAN: *(To Penny.)* Why thank you, cupcake.

CARA: I can't believe . . .

MAGGIE: What? That I'm wearing a hand-me-down?

CARA: That you're wearing a hand-me-down that you stole from Jonathan's trash!

MAGGIE: So what if I am? It was just sitting there on top. A perfectly good shirt going to waste. Any of you would have done the same thing.

JONATHAN: Look, Maggie. There's nothing wrong with wearing that shirt. Well . . . there is, but that's another story.

MAGGIE: I know . . . but . . . so what?

JONATHAN: BUT, there is something wrong with you openly laughing at Cara. Sure, Cara's nose isn't perfect . . .

PENNY: Jono!

JONATHAN: Well, it's not! *(To Cara.)* Sorry, Care.

CARA: It's OK Jono.

JONATHAN: But she's a great person, so who cares what her nose looks like. I mean, come on Maggie. You have her thinking she's a little winged creature of some sort.

PENNY: *(Laughing.)* Yeah . . . she thinks she's as bad as Tucci, the dog-faced boy.

MAGGIE: No one's as bad as Tucci.

CARA: Thank you. Look, Maggie, I know what it's like to wear hand-me-downs and I know what it's like to have to wear the same skirt three days in a row because you simply don't have anything else, but do you know what it's like to wake up every morning with a big nose?

MAGGIE: Actually, I don't think your nose is that big. I just . . . I saw the girls looking at the shirt, and out of sheer paranoia, I quickly changed the subject. *(Pause.)* I really don't know why I did that.

PENNY: I do.

JONATHAN: *(To Penny.)* Silence is a virtue.

MAGGIE: Listen, Cara, I'm so sorry. Really. I don't have a lot of people I can depend on, but I know you're always there, and I don't know what I'd do if that ever changed. *(Pause.)* Please, Cara. Please forgive me.

CARA: Of course, Maggie. Just never do that to . . .

MAGGIE: Never.

CARA: To me or anyone ever again.

MAGGIE: Not even Tucci?

CARA: *(Smiling.)* Well . . . maybe Tucci. No, no, no . . . not even Tucci!

MAGGIE: OK.

JONATHAN: Super!

PENNY: Thank God.

CARA: All right you guys. Let's go to lunch.

JONATHAN: Sounds fantastic. Can we go to this great little place that my mom showed me?

PENNY: No.

JONATHAN: *(Upset.)* Why not?

PENNY: Because . . .

JONATHAN: No one even likes you Penny.

(Cara laughs at Penny and Jonathan as they exit the bathroom. Maggie and Cara turn and smile at each other one last time.)

END OF PLAY

RIDING NOWHERE FAST

2F

By Erica Burroughs
San Clemente, California

Characters

SHELBY
CLARE

Setting

Shelby and Cassidy are cycling side-by-side on stationary bikes. They ride these bikes throughout the entire play.

RIDING NOWHERE FAST

At rise, at a gym.

SHELBY: If we keep this up, if we do this every single day, we'll be babes by the summer.

CASSIDY: I don't know if I can do this every single day. It's so boring. Aren't you bored?

SHELBY: You're bored? I'm not bored. I'm talking to you. We're having a nice conversation. Are you saying you think you're boring? Are you saying *I'm* boring?

CASSIDY: It's hard to talk and ride at the same time. I need air.

SHELBY: It's good to talk and ride at the same time. You're burning more calories.

CASSIDY: Do you think I'm fat?

SHELBY: Not at all. Not one little bit. But you're gonna look so much better in a bathing suit by working out every day, don't you agree?

CASSIDY: I guess. *(Pause. They pedal in silence for a moment.)* You're so motivated.

SHELBY: I am. It's in my genes.

CASSIDY: Your genes?

SHELBY: Yup . . . everyone in my family is motivated. My dad. Totally motivated. Super-attorney. Never loses a case. God help us all if he does. Mom. Ad exec — extraordinaire. Every campaign she creates is a surefire hit. And my sister, as you know . . .

CASSIDY: She should win a gold medal. Amazing gymnast. She really is amazing.

SHELBY: She is. She knows it too. But see . . . my entire family . . . they're all a bunch of overachievers. I have to be too, to keep up.

CASSIDY: It's a lot of pressure.

SHELBY: Tell me about it.

CASSIDY: I'm not that motivated.

SHELBY: Yeah, you are.

CASSIDY: No . . . I'm really not. I'm really very lazy.

SHELBY: Well, you're here, aren't you?

CASSIDY: Honestly, I'm hating this.

SHELBY: You think I like it?

CASSIDY: Yeah, you seem to.

SHELBY: I hate it too.

CASSIDY: Really?

SHELBY: But I can't *not* do it, ya know what I mean?

CASSIDY: I guess. I like the results, that's for sure.

SHELBY: That's what I'm talking about. That's one good thing I learned from my dad. To focus on the goal. "If you focus on the goal, the task itself doesn't seem as insurmountable."

CASSIDY: You sounded just like your dad.

SHELBY: I know. I do a great impression of him.

CASSIDY: My dad never tells me cool stuff like that.

SHELBY: Well, I'm happy to pass on all my dad's words of wisdom. It gets kind of obnoxious sometimes.

CASSIDY: But still . . . it's helping you now. It's helping you get here every day.

SHELBY: Yeah . . . if he only knew that my goal in life is to look good in a bathing suit this summer, I'm not sure he'd be too happy.

CASSIDY: He should be happy that you have a goal at all.

SHELBY: Totally!

(*Pause as they ride in silence for a moment.*)

CASSIDY: So, what happens after?

SHELBY: After what?

CASSIDY: After we reach our goal?

SHELBY: Oh. Ummm . . . we get another one.

CASSIDY: Would that include going to the gym every day?

SHELBY: That depends on what the goal is.

CASSIDY: I guess.

SHELBY: But once you look great in a bathing suit, you can't just stop. I mean, you have to keep it up.

CASSIDY: Oh, no. Really?

SHELBY: Well, maybe not every day. But Cass, it's hard work looking good. It takes every ounce of your focus and discipline. And once you actually do look good, you can't let it slip away. So it takes extra amounts of focus and discipline. It's actually harder to keep it, then to get it.

CASSIDY: Oh, my God. You're totally freaking me out. You're saying that for the rest of my life, I have to spend seven days in the gym riding this stupid thing? I'm exhausted.

SHELBY: Well, if you want, we can do the Stairmaster tomorrow instead.

CASSIDY: Whoopee! That's something to look forward to.

SHELBY: Cassidy, I thought I was helping you out. You're my best friend, and I thought I was doing you a favor. But if it's too much for you, then don't come. And don't blame me when guys are staring at me all summer long, and you look like the Pillsbury Doughboy.

CASSIDY: You just said you didn't think I was fat.

SHELBY: I'm sorry. You're not. But you are really white. Next thing we need to do is work on your tan.

CASSIDY: It's so bad for you. Tans are bad for you.

SHELBY: But it looks so good. And having a tan makes you look even thinner.

CASSIDY: It does not.

SHELBY: Of course it does. Everyone knows that.

CASSIDY: Wow. There's a lot of work to be done.

SHELBY: We'll get there. I know we will. But you can't poop out on me.

CASSIDY: I'm here, aren't I?

SHELBY: Good girl.

(They pedal in silence for a moment.)

CASSIDY: Don't you think it's weird?

SHELBY: What's weird?

CASSIDY: That riding bikes that take us nowhere is our goal.

SHELBY: That's not our goal. Looking good is our goal.

CASSIDY: We're spinning into infinity.

SHELBY: We're spinning into a bikini.

CASSIDY: I don't even care about that.

SHELBY: You will in July.

CASSIDY: It feels like we should have more important goals.

SHELBY: Like what?

CASSIDY: I don't know. Saving the earth from destruction?

SHELBY: Honestly, Cassidy, how are we going to do that? If you want to achieve your goal, you need to make it an attainable one. My dad told me that too.

CASSIDY: Your dad just keeps 'em coming, doesn't he?

SHELBY: You should live with him. Every single word out of his mouth is some "pearl of wisdom."

CASSIDY: Well, don't you think saving the earth is an attainable goal?

SHELBY: Not by July.

CASSIDY: So, in July, when we're laying on the beach in our bikinis all tan and thin and gorgeous, having guys gawk at us, then and only then, we can concentrate on saving the earth?

SHELBY: Sure. Why not? We can start by strutting down the beach and picking up garbage. A good way to not only show off our new figures, but to keep them too!

CASSIDY: Well, that's good. And at least we'll be walking somewhere. Not just riding down the road to nowhere.

SHELBY: I keep telling you Cass, it's not riding to nowhere . . . it's riding to our goal. It might feel like nowhere right now . . . but just wait and see. I have a feeling you're going to thank me.

CASSIDY: I'll thank you when we're actually cleaning up the beach and doing something worthwhile.

SHELBY: Fair enough.

(They pedal in silence for a moment.)

CASSIDY: How close to being done are we?

SHELBY: Soon, Cass. Maybe another fifteen minutes.

CASSIDY: And then we do it all over again tomorrow.

SHELBY: Yup.

CASSIDY: I'm not gonna talk now. I'm not gonna talk for the next fifteen minutes. I need my oxygen.

SHELBY: That's fine. You've burned plenty of calories today Cass. You did really well. I'm proud of you.

CASSIDY: Thanks. I'm not talking.

SHELBY: Tomorrow we'll do the Stairmaster. We'll climb those stairs for sixty minutes. We'll climb those stairs to achieve our goal. Our beautiful, bikini-clad, environmentalist goal! OK? *(Cassidy doesn't answer.)* OK? *(No answer.)* That's right. You're not talking. Well, just keep pedaling, Cass. Keep pedaling!

END OF PLAY

WOODSMAN JACK

5M

By Alyssa Hood
Santa Margarita Catholic High School
Rancho Santa Margarita, California

Characters

JACE: A pale young man with blond hair, a genuine smile, and long limbs. He is incredibly witty.

COLLIN: Medium in height with a brown curly mop of hair. "The glass is half empty but only because I drank some" kind of guy.

DREW: Taller than the rest, with straight black hair and black-rimmed glasses. The dreamer who makes any decision wholeheartedly.

TODD: The smallest one in the group. Longish brown hair and a navy blue hat with a yellow "M" that stands for Michigan, even though he is a native of Connecticut.

THE MAN: An ominous, mysterious figure.

Setting

Late at night in the woods. Four boys, all around seventeen, are sitting on logs around a campfire.

WOODSMAN JACK

Scene 1

JACE: All right, I have a true story . . .

COLLIN: Oh, come on Jace. You? A *true* story?
    (All boys, except Jace, laugh.)

JACE: No, really. I'm serious. Have any of you ever heard of Woodsman Jack?

DREW: Woodsman Jack? Who's that?

JACE: Woodsman Jack was a camp counselor at this very camp around ten years ago. He was great with kids and everyone loved him. Then one day, they say he just snapped and threw a kid off the porch of Cabin Sixteen. Once he realized what he had done, he took off into the woods and lives in some mobile home, not far from here.

TODD: Woodsman Jack is a myth. My sister told me that story when I was eleven. Not real, man.

JACE: Guys, guys, c'mon. It's true.

COLLIN: Prove it, Jace.

DREW: Yeah.

TODD: Prove it, man.

JACE: *(Standing up.)* Fine. Tomorrow after lunch . . . we find his trailer. *(He exits.)*

DREW: You don't think we'll find anything, do you?

TODD: No way man.

DREW: Ten bucks says we do.

COLLIN: Ten bucks we don't.

DREW and COLLIN: You're on!
    (Blackout.)

Scene 2

The boys meet outside of the mess hall.

JACE: You *girls* ready?

TODD: Yeah.

COLLIN: Sure.

DREW: Whatever.

(They head into the woods. After a while, they find a trailer.)

TODD: No way . . .

COLLIN: This doesn't prove anything yet.

JACE: Ha, ha! You see?

(Jace and Drew smile at each other and are the first to reach the trailer. Jace opens the door slowly and steps inside with the others following.)

DREW: Hello . . . ?

COLLIN: See . . . there's nobody here. It's just a trailer in the woods. Let's go. And Drew, you owe me ten bucks.

JACE: Not so fast . . .

(Jace heads toward the back of the trailer. There is a closed door. He slowly reaches out and flings open the door. A hissing cat is heard. Jace and the others jump back.)

TODD: Whoa!

(A groan comes from inside the room, and a figure stumbles to the doorway.)

COLLIN: Let's . . .

TODD: get . . .

DREW: out of . . .

JACE: HERE!

(The boys run for the door. Collin, Drew, and Jace make it out. Jace slams the door behind him leaving Todd inside. The boys run for it, but Collin suddenly stops.)

COLLIN: Where's Todd?

DREW: I dunno.

(Collin runs back to the trailer and pulls Todd out. They continue running. As they run, Collin's wallet falls from his pocket. Blackout.)

SCENE 3

The boys are running back toward camp with the "figure" not far behind them.

TODD: Head for that shed over there.
  (The boys run faster toward the shed and all duck inside.)
COLLIN: *(Out of breath.)* Do you think we lost him?
  (Jace pops his head out of the shed, then turns back to his friends.)
JACE: Yeah, I think so.
DREW: Good. Hey, Collin?
COLLIN: Yeah?
DREW: You owe me ten bucks.
COLLIN: Aw, come off it Drew. Can we do this later?
DREW: No. I want my ten dollars now. Otherwise, you'll tell me I already gave it to you or something like that, and I won't ever get it.
TODD: Yeah, Collin, pay up.
JACE: Guys, not now. Come on . . . be quiet. I think he's coming.
  (Hurried footsteps are heard, and a shadow appears. The figure walks up to the doorway of the shed. All the boys scream wildly and cover their faces. Man walks up to Collin.)
MAN: Young sir . . . I believe you dropped your wallet.
  (Man puts the wallet in Collin's hand.)
MAN: There you go . . . be careful with that.
COLLIN: Th . . . th . . . .thanks.
  (Man walks back toward the woods and disappears from sight.)
DREW: Hey Collin?
COLLIN: Yeah?
DREW: Now that you have your wallet back, can I have my ten bucks?

END OF PLAY